A	B	C	D	E	F	G	H

I	J	K	L	M	N	P	Q
						52	

SPECIAL NEEDS UNIT 01902 556256

Thembelani Ngenelwa

THE DAY I DIED

Kwela Books

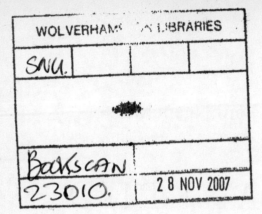
Kwela Books,
a division of NB Publishers (Pty) Limited,
40 Heerengracht, Cape Town, South Africa
PO Box 6525, Roggebaai, 8012, South Africa
http://www.kwela.com

Copyright © 2007 T. Ngenelwa

Cover photographs by Nick Aldridge
Cover design by Nita Nagar, Oryx Media Productions
Typography by Nazli Jacobs
Set in Plantin
Printed and bound by Paarl Print,
Oosterland Street, Paarl, South Africa

First edition, first impression 2007

ISBN-10: 0-7957-0244-2
ISBN-13: 978-0-7957-0244-0

This book is dedicated to the memory of
my late beloved father, Malusi Jackson Ngenelwa,
and to my daughter, Emihle.
The time between the death of my father and the
birth of my daughter made me appreciate the
greatest gift I have: life.

My first steps

I was born and grew up near a small place called Engcobo, in the Eastern Cape. Engcobo is a small rural town in the former Transkei and it was there that I grew up as a barefoot boy who took pride in herding his father's livestock. My village was called eMadladleni and we used to herd our parents' cattle on the banks of Umgwali river. In this place I grew up knowing that a stranger is a friend that you haven't met yet.

Life was very simple in eMadladleni, but we were encouraged to go to school as teachers were the only professionals in the area, and our parents had dreams of us growing up to become successful people. My parents used to reward me by slaughtering a sheep in my honour for every year of school that I managed to pass. When I passed with a distinction they would buy me a new pair of shoes and treat me to a holiday at my maternal grandmother's place. This would mean a double celebration, as my granny would also slaughter a sheep for her intelligent grandson.

We were a very loving and close-knit family that valued life and appreciated the little that we had. We were also very religious, with my father being an evangelist in the local United Methodist Church of Southern Africa. He was a well-known, loved and respected preacher. In fact, both my parents and grandparents were very good community and church members.

Growing up in such a religious family had its pressures as well

as its rewards. Although our parents didn't believe in forcing us to go to church, as they believed that we would go when we wanted to, there was no question that we were expected to grow up to be responsible members of the community and church like our parents. My family were hoping that maybe my two brothers and I would even go one step further than our father and become priests.

My resemblance to my father and my status as a first-born son didn't help to ease this pressure. In fact, the expectations kind of stifled me. I was determined that I was an individual, not just an extension of my parents. Because of this pressure I didn't pay much attention to religion, even though I came from such a family. We were always taught never to stop praying and trusting in God, but I thought of a prayer as part of a routine rather than a sacred communication with God. I took everything for granted and never took time to think about my relationship with Him. I only prayed when I had to, and once I was away from my parents I would be like any other naughty boy. The only church services I ever went to were the ones that took place at night and the only reason I went was to check out the girls. So it is correct to say that I understood religion but never believed in it.

When I went to Manzana High School in 1992, I chose Mathematics and Physical Science as my major subjects because I had this dream of becoming a doctor one day. As I have mentioned, there were very few professions that we knew about in our village: everyone wanted to be a doctor, a nurse or a teacher.

While I was studying at high school I stayed in a rented hostel for boys as the school was far from my village. It was here that I learned to be independent and where I also learned some undesirable habits. I was fifteen, very short and very talkative, and I quickly became popular for all the wrong reasons.

At home I had always been secretly rebellious. For instance, I would often sneak out at night to attend parties. To do this I would go to bed as early as half past seven in the evening so that nobody would suspect anything and then get up when my parents went to sleep. I would come home early in the morning and, by the time they got up, I would be busy pretending to be cleaning the hut that I slept in.

But at high school there were very few people who knew my parents and I knew that whatever happened at high school would remain there. I quickly attracted a string of friends and girlfriends and started experimenting with cigarettes and alcohol. The fact of the matter is that I was just like every other teenage boy. I was subjected to the same peer pressure that every boy my age was subjected to. I knew my parents' expectations but I was too busy rebelling.

Despite this, I wasn't all bad: I was very good with my books, I respected society – especially the elders, as our culture dictates – and I had never failed a single class in my life.

I made some life changes when I got to matric in 1994, chose different friends and focused on my schooling. The possibility of success through education was becoming a reality; I was just one year from university. I started to be more careful about my actions and studied very hard that year even though I was struggling financially.

My father was the breadwinner and the money that he sent

home at the end of the month wasn't enough to sustain my family and pay for my high-school expenses. Our hostel was self-catering and that made things even more difficult. Nonetheless, I was determined to study hard and pass.

At the end of that year, despite struggling financially, I managed to pass my matric with an exemption. My family slaughtered a sheep and invited the relatives and neighbours to celebrate my achievement. I was the pride of the entire community as I was the only one in our village who was sitting matric that year. I also happened to be the first member of my family to achieve an exemption and this made it even more special.

However, in our school there was no career guidance or advice about post-matric education and so I didn't manage to study in 1995. This was, in part, because my parents didn't have enough money to pay my fees that year, but it was mainly due to a lack of information that I hadn't applied for a bursary or any form of financial assistance.

I used that year to do some research about courses and to apply for bursaries and find some work so that I could save up some money for the following year. The following year, 1996, I enrolled with the University of the Western Cape in Bellville for a BSc degree.

From Cape Town to Jozi

I made a lot of friends at university and I enjoyed my life there, but my best friend was Khaya Bolosha. We had a lot in common and we both tended to find humour in everything. Our problems seemed to be similar too, especially because we both came from poor families. I remember one year, when I was struggling with paying the residence fees, Khaya offered to share his residence room with me. We shared his room for an entire year. The following year, Khaya had the same problem when he lost his partial bursary and was forced out of the residence. That year I had a room and naturally we shared my room. At the time I secretly celebrated his financial problem because it gave me a chance to pay him back for his good deed the previous year.

By the time he completed his studies we had grown to love each other like brothers and when he moved to Johannesburg, to look for work, we agreed that I would visit any time I wanted.

I did pretty well at my studies, even though finances were tight, and after completing my studies at UWC I was offered a job by the university as an IT technical assistant. The university offered me a job because of my work ethic and the skills I had developed during my days as a student assistant in the university computer labs. However, my contract was going to expire at the end of 2003. I had to apply for other jobs so that when the contract expired I had something to fall back on.

Khaya had looked for a job for two years in Cape Town after he had graduated, but it was only after he moved to Johannesburg that he found a good job. This prompted me to consider looking for a job in Gauteng as well.

I had been to Johannesburg for the first time in 2000. I had gone there primarily to visit my friends Khaya and Siviwe, but I also wanted to see that side of the country and satisfy my curiosity about Jozi.

The first time I had visited Khaya in Jo'burg I had been blown away by the vibrancy of such a big city. I had stayed with him in Goodhope Extension 5 (affectionately known just as Five), an informal settlement just outside of Germiston, and had visited the suburbs on the weekends to see my other friends and former classmates.

Job seeking had not been top of my agenda at the time, as I was still hopeful of landing something in Cape Town, but now, in 2003, things had changed: I needed a good job and I needed it immediately. My father was unemployed as the asbestos factory he had worked at for thirty years had closed down. He had been the sole breadwinner in my family ever since I was born, but the meagre sum of money that he had received from the factory was already dwindling. My mother brought in some money by selling fruit and fast-food snacks at a local school, but it wasn't enough to sustain a family of seven. I had vowed to find work and put an end to my family's sufferings. I knew their expectations and I wanted to meet them.

I had decided to ask for three weeks' leave at the end of September 2003, so that I could visit my friends in Jo'burg and look for a job. I am a person who really believes in loyalty. I was loyal to UWC – after all, they gave me my very first pay cheque – but staying in Cape Town hadn't turned out to be the right option and I had to look elsewhere. I was more than ready for the journey.

I went to the Bellville train station with my girlfriend, Cynthia, who had bought me a ticket the previous day. As we hugged she whispered, "Good luck, take care of yourself."

Then she turned away and didn't turn back as she left the station; she didn't want me to see her in tears.

Inside the train I shared a compartment with five other people. I was the only stranger among them, but they tried their best to welcome me and make me feel at ease. They were a gentleman in his early forties and his wife, a guy my age, a boy in his early teens and a lady in her early thirties. I sat next to the window to enjoy the view and get some fresh air.

I had bought two magazines in Bellville to prepare for a twenty-seven hour journey to Johannesburg, so I wasn't worried about being bored, but with five other nice people in the compartment I had absolutely nothing to worry about, least of all boredom. The compartment was filled with their fun and laughter and very soon I started chatting to them. They were all on their way back to Pretoria; they had been in Cape Town for a family holiday.

The journey was long and tiresome, but we kept ourselves entertained by singing. I was burning with anticipation and, to ease the tension, I was frequently on the phone to update the guys about my journey.

Each station we stopped at brought more eagerness and excitement, but it was only late the next morning that the stations began to become more frequent as we neared Jo'burg. As midday approached I looked through the window when the train slowed down and saw Randfontein station. At that moment I felt even more excited because I knew that we would soon be arriving at Johannesburg station.

As we approached Johannesburg I began to see some familiar places. I could see the skyscrapers from a distance. "Jo'burg, here I come," I thought quietly to myself. I couldn't help smiling.

It was around two in the afternoon when the Shosholoza Meyl train finally arrived at Johannesburg Park station. The station was just as overcrowded as the last time I had been there and people, as always, looked very happy. Jo'burg was warm and sunny; it was the perfect spring day. I stuck my head out of the window to get a better view and the air blew on my face coolly as if to welcome me. We were finally there.

After stopping briefly at Johannesburg station, the train pulled off once more and headed for Germiston and the East Rand.

When the train got to Germiston station I peeped through the window to try to spot the people who had come to fetch me. You must remember that the last time I had been in Johannesburg my friends were staying in a shack in Five. Since then they had moved to a flat in town and somebody would have to be at the station to fetch me and to show me where they stayed. Still looking through that train window, I heard a familiar voice calling my name. It was Zolisa, one of my friends from Germiston. I noticed that he had picked up a little weight but other than that he was the same old Zolisa with his ever-expanding bald patch. He was in his early thirties but had the energy of a twenty-year-old. He was with two other friends that I didn't know at the time, but I soon learnt that they were Khaya's friends whom he had told me about over the phone. One was particularly short with long ears and big eyes. The guy was slightly built but looked very strong. His name was Bongani; he was about my age, but with a lighter complexion than mine. The other one was bigger than Bongani but looked younger. He must have been in his late teens. His name was Dumisa.

As we walked together from the train they kept making jokes and asking why I had picked up so much weight. Here we were, strangers, but chatting as if we'd known each other for ever. We just clicked from the moment we met. It was a meeting of like minds and characters. I quickly figured out that Khaya had told them about all my tricks and habits because they asked me about the things that I did while Khaya and I were still living in Cape Town. The guys had never been to Cape Town and they were eager to know about life in the Cape because the only things they knew came from watching television. As we walked I told them about the beauty of Cape Town.

They took me to a tall, pink block of flats on Station Road called Pirrowville. It was a beautiful new block and Khaya's apartment was on the ground floor. I was struck by the contrast between the apartment and the simple shack he had lived in at Five. It was a big change and though I was impressed by the new place, I also knew that it would never be the same as the township life that had become so familiar to me while I was living in Five.

When Khaya arrived from work that evening, he was just the same old Khaya. He was exactly the same height as I was, of an ebony colour and a gym enthusiast. He had a boyish voice and would laugh every time I tried to dance – he thought I was the worst dancer ever and he was not that far from the truth.

Khaya was sharing the flat with Zolisa and Bongani. Khanyisa, Khaya's younger brother, was also staying there while the schools were on holiday. After the others went to bed Khaya and I chatted until early in the morning, updating each other about the changes in Johannesburg and Cape Town and making plans to reintroduce me to Jozi.

The following day was a Saturday and no-one had to go to work. We visited shopping malls and went to a party in one of the flats in town. It was so good that I didn't miss Cape Town once.

The whole first week was filled with humour and excitement, but even though there was a lot of partying I didn't once forget what had brought me to Gauteng. I would buy a train ticket into town every day and visit all the employment agencies, drop my CV and sometimes approach Human Resources managers directly. I had to find a job and I had to find it immediately. Every single day presented its own challenges as far as job seeking was concerned, but there was no way I was prepared to go back to Cape Town without the good news my family needed to hear. I was going to do everything it took to find a job and even though I was really enjoying the life in Germiston, without the worry of waking up in the morning to go to work, it was all about getting a job.

The day

It's amazing how you sometimes wake up feeling so good about yourself for no particular reason. It's a feeling that takes you through the day and makes you excited about life. On Wednesday, 1 October 2003, I woke up feeling like this.

At about half past eight I jumped out of bed, looking forward to the day ahead. The guys had already all gone to work, leaving only Bongani, Khanyisa and myself in the flat, and it was quiet as the other two were still sleeping.

I stepped outside and felt the warm Johannesburg sunshine, took a deep breath of morning air and told myself that this would be a good day for me. Then I looked up at the sky. It was clear but there was one little dark cloud that hung there like a misplaced dirty sock in the kitchen. This little cloud was starting to spread and it was spoiling what was otherwise promising to be a beautiful day. In our culture they regard a dark cloud as a sign that somebody is about to die, but it is also a clear sign that it is about to rain and rain is a symbol of new life. Because of this I didn't know how to interpret the sky and went inside.

I had called my parents the previous day to let them know that I was in Johannesburg. They knew my reasons and never had a problem with my being in Jozi as they knew my friends. My mother had answered the phone. Usually she is always happy to hear my voice over the phone, but this particular day she didn't sound

17

happy at all, even though I had recently deposited some money for her. In fact, she sounded very worried.

"Sisi, you sound uncomfortable, is there anything bothering you?" I asked.

"Nothing, mntwan'am, there is no problem with me, just look very well after yourself whilst you are still there," she replied.

However, even though my mother didn't seem happy, she wished me well in my endeavours and thanked me for the money that I had deposited for them. I knew that I had her blessings and prayers. I had an urge to talk to my father and my brothers as well, but my mother was the only one at home so I said my good-byes.

After speaking to my mother I had gone to the employment agencies again to see if they didn't have any more vacancies. By this stage I had managed to secure an appointment with an IT manager from one of the companies I had visited in Kempton Park. The appointment for an interview was scheduled for that coming Friday. I was really looking forward to impressing them, but that didn't mean that I could stop looking.

After I had finished at the last agency I decided to go to Wits University and visit their careers centre. I was hoping to get some advice. That is where I met Mthetho, a friend who had also stud-ied at UWC. He was working as a clinical psychologist and lecturer. He took me to his office, where we chatted for hours, reminiscing about our days back in the Cape and our future ambitions. We shared a common goal, that of putting our humble backgrounds behind us and putting our beloved Eastern Cape on the map.

I had really enjoyed seeing the success that Mthetho had made of himself, but Tuesday had been a busy day and I had decided to take it easy that Wednesday morning. Bongani wanted to take a stroll into town and visit his girlfriend who stayed in a small suburb called Delville, on the outskirts of Germiston, and I decided to go with him.

On our way back, I received a call from my friend who stayed in Five. She asked me when I was planning to visit them, so I told her that I would as soon as my friends came back from work. I was keen to see Five again because the first time I had visited Gauteng, in 2000, I had shared a two-bedroom shack there with Khaya, Siviwe and Zolisa. Five was the first place that I had known in Gauteng and I had made lots of friends in the area. The place was a hive of activity and the people were so positive about life despite their circumstances. People came from all walks of life, with different cultures and languages, but they all mingled together and took care of one another. They would call one another makhi, meaning "good neighbour", and everyone knew everyone else.

I remember one day while I was staying there, the community had gathered to support one boy who had passed his matric with an exemption. The young man's parents could never afford to send him to university, but the community had managed to raise some funds to send the boy to study further.

It is true that there were also a lot of shebeens in Five, but I hardly saw any crime of any kind amongst the community members and, in all the days that I stayed there, I don't remember seeing any violence. There was always a good atmosphere in the area, so good in fact that you would go to town and rush back as soon as you finished your shopping just to enjoy the place. You didn't have to wait for an invitation to go to any party in the neighbourhood, you could just rock up and the partygoers would just welcome and entertain you. The people were true to themselves and nobody looked down on anyone else.

So you must understand that this place was very close to my heart. I felt that for me to feel like I had really arrived in Gauteng, I had to shake the hands of our ex-neighbours and old friends. It would be some sort of homecoming. I would also get a chance to see some people from my beloved Engcobo who stayed there. All of my friends in Germiston originally came from the other areas of the Eastern Cape, so I was really excited about seeing my abakhaya.

Bongani and I decided to cook so that by the time the guys got back from work the food would be ready. This way they wouldn't waste time; they'd just have their meals and we would head straight to the township.

We had also been invited to a party in one of the flats in Germiston, so we decided we would go to Five first and attend the party later. We knew that we would visit the township again at the weekend, and probably spend the whole of Saturday afternoon there, so it didn't matter that this was going to be a short visit. I decided on the easiest of meals: mince mixed with potatoes. I knew that this wouldn't take too long to make and wouldn't expose my cooking skills, or lack thereof – I am also not the greatest cook on earth.

Round about five in the afternoon Khaya and Zolisa arrived from work. Khaya, in particular, was so excited about visiting Five that he ended up eating only half of his meal. Strangely, though, Zolisa didn't want to go to Five, claiming that he was utterly exhausted from work. I call this strange because he was usually the first to want to visit somewhere, even if he didn't know the people we were visiting. Sometimes he would even volunteer to pay the taxi fare, but on this day, when we wanted to go to a place that was only walking distance away, the place that he knew better than any of us, he just didn't feel like going.

Khaya's younger brother, Khanyisa, also wanted to come with us. We usually let him come along, but that afternoon I just didn't want him there. I told him he had to stay behind and wait until we came back, telling him that we would go to the flat party together later.

I still don't know why I refused to let him come with us when even his elder brother wanted him to tag along. I suppose I didn't want this young "laaitie" spoiling the big boys' fun.

While Khaya and Bongani did everything in a hurry I went upstairs to the public phones to confirm that we were on our way. Then Khaya, Bongani and I were in the street, greeting our friends as we passed with smiles as wide as the Amazon river.

Since it was getting colder, I had taken Bongani's green jacket. I hadn't brought any warm clothing with me as I had expected Johannesburg to be very hot around October time. Underneath Bongani's jacket I was only wearing the black tracksuit I usually wore for our daily jogs. I had decided to look as ordinary as possible, so that I wouldn't attract any attention. We had also decided to leave our cellphones and all our important possessions behind, in case we got robbed or something bad happened.

We went past the big Enterprise meat factory, heading for the industrial area near the railway lines. The area was so quiet that we could hear our own footsteps. We were walking fast because it was getting colder, busy cracking jokes and reminiscing about the last time we were all in Five together.

Soon we could see a few shacks and, as we went closer, we left the main road and took a path that would take us straight to the township. On either side of the path, the grass was overgrown and dry. There was a railway bridge on our right-hand side and to get to the township we had to walk alongside the bridge and across the railway lines.

As we approached the bridge, we came across five guys who were going towards the area we were coming from. I was walking behind Bongani and Khaya because they were more familiar with the path than I was, so I never really bothered to look at the other guys' faces. I didn't see any need to do so. We were just going our way, minding our own business. They were also going their own way, minding their own business. That's what I kept telling myself but, in all honesty, I sensed danger.

As they approached, they seemed to be engaged in conversation. You could see this from the way the one in front kept looking behind to check on the others. He was wearing a maroon T-shirt and khaki Dickies pants. Strangely enough, he was the only one that I seemed to notice. Somehow he looked like the leader of the group. I cannot remember a single thing about the rest of them. This guy just stood out, for whatever reason.

"Hola, bafethu," they greeted us as they passed by.

We returned the greeting and they continued with their journey, but I must admit that after those guys had passed I had an uneasy feeling once more and my heart started pumping faster.

I'm not usually someone who scares easily, but that day I just felt afraid. I couldn't help having a quick look back, just to check that they weren't up to something, just to be sure, but when I glanced over my shoulder they were just continuing with their journey towards town.

Reassured, I tried to concentrate on the conversation we were having. Neither Khaya nor Bongani seemed bothered about anything and I didn't want to be seen as the scared little guy from Cape Town. After all, I had been to Five before and I had also been to a lot of supposedly dangerous townships in Cape Town. I didn't fear any township.

We crossed the railway lines and entered the settlement. I felt relieved as we approached and we all started walking a little faster now we were on more familiar ground.

I smiled as I saw the shacks; some people had made their homes from planks and some from corrugated iron, but all of the shacks had been painted in different colours. I loved the assortment of colours that they boasted. But it was also obvious that the place had changed a lot. There was a big empty space behind the township that had once housed many people. Most of the shacks had been removed; presumably the owners had been moved to the new RDP houses in other areas. The shacks that used to be next to ours were no longer there, but I noticed a green shack that I recognised, opposite the water tap we used back in 2000. People were still fetching water from the same tap.

We went past a spaza whose owner used to call me mkhaya,

since he was originally from Engcobo. We asked the shopkeeper about him, but he told us he was the new owner as the previous owner had sold the shop and moved to a different area.

Finally we saw the blue shack we were looking for. We knocked at the open door and found Nomaphelo and her cousin, who was visiting from East London, inside. As soon as we were in, she made a phone call and within minutes Mheza came in with a wide smile that went from ear to ear. I started laughing out loud when he started his trademark "salute", but at first he didn't recognise me as the light wasn't bright enough. That was until I called him Mathintitha, the pet name I had given him back in 2000. Then he knew who I was immediately and shouted back, "Young boy, are you back from the Cape?"

We shook hands and started chatting. Mheza had a stutter, yet he wanted us to listen to him all the time. He was even more excited when he saw me as he wasn't aware that I was in town. We started reminiscing about the last time I was there and it was nice. Then they began to tell us of how the place had changed and how dangerous it had become. When I asked about my abakhaya I was informed that they had moved to the nearby area called Rondebult.

After chatting to Mheza we decided to leave early so that we could get back to Germiston for the flat party and he could attend a memorial service for a lady who had been stabbed to death, apparently by a jealous boyfriend. Nomaphelo asked if she could come with us so that she could see where we stayed. We had already told her about the party in town that we were all going to, so she decided she'd rather go with us because she was not going to go to work the following day. We said our goodbyes to Mheza while we waited for Nomaphelo to put on her jacket and then headed home the same way we had come.

We meet again

We made our way through the labyrinth of shacks, the only light coming from a single lamppost about two hundred metres away. I couldn't believe that it had become so dark after such a short period of time. It was so dark that it was difficult for me to even see the path in front of me.

The path wound between the shacks in a way that meant you wouldn't know which way to go to avoid bumping into someone coming the other way. I remembered though, from my stay there in 2000, that the locals didn't seem to mind the inconvenience; they would just squeeze past and continue on their way.

This was not the only way to town. There was another path on the other side of the township that would take us directly onto the main road, but we had all decided that it was too long; the weather was starting to feel colder and we wanted to get home as soon as possible. I had Bongani's light jacket on and it wasn't helping at all; it felt like a shirt.

So we had decided to take the short cut, the path we had used to get to the township in the first place. Nomaphelo told me not to worry about anything as this path was used by the workers from the Enterprise butchery on their way to and from work, especially by those who worked night shifts, but, surprisingly for such a busy path, we didn't come across a single soul. Was it because of the funeral service that Mheza was attending? I asked myself.

The road seemed longer this time, but I thought that I would feel better once we had crossed the railway lines and were nearer the factories; at least by then we would be closer to home.

As we left the township we could see the lights of cars on the main road ahead, but between them and us there was deserted land which was very dark. The lights from the factories near the main road were our only hope of seeing where we were going.

At that moment I decided that while we might be frightened in the township – myself at least – there was absolutely nothing to fear in front of us as the big factory buildings always had security guards. The only people we were likely to see coming from that direction at that time were workers from the Enterprise butchery. No-one would be coming from town as it was a little late and the shops would have all closed at around six.

The four of us walked for about fifty metres along the dark path. Khaya was complaining that he was hungry, he had eaten only half of his meal, and we knew that with Zolisa and Khanyisa in the flat there would be nothing left of the food by the time we got home.

Suddenly our conversation about the cold temperature and the food was disturbed and for the first time I wasn't the only scared person in the group.

There in front of us were five figures. Upon closer inspection, they looked like the people we had seen earlier on. The strange thing is that we didn't see them approaching us; they just seemed to appear out of nowhere. Three of them had appeared out of the darkness on our left and the other two on our right. Had they been hiding in the shrubs? There was no time to ask.

We soon noticed that they really were the same guys who had greeted us earlier on, but now they seemed to be restless. They seemed to be looking for something on the path.

Because the path wasn't wide enough, we were walking in pairs; Khaya and Bongani in the front, Nomaphelo and myself behind them. There was no turning back; we had to walk on, but without provoking them. All of a sudden my friends and I looked very small and vulnerable. Time froze as I kept my eye on Nomaphelo, who was by my side, because I thought she would be the easiest target.

We braved it, though, and walked through them without saying anything. I breathed a sigh of relief when they didn't block our way. As we moved on I listened for their footsteps but I couldn't hear a thing, a clear indication that they hadn't continued towards the township. We started to walk a little faster. The frequency of Bongani's footsteps increased. My heart began to beat as if it would pop out of my chest.

The distance between Khaya and Bongani and Nomaphelo and myself was starting to widen. We were all starting to breathe heavily and it must have been clear how scared we were.

At that moment Nomaphelo bumped into me and I stumbled but did not fall. I tried to say something but my throat was just too dry, no words would come out. My right leg bumped against something in the dark and I staggered but just managed to regain my balance. My frightened eyes reached for Khaya and I saw him also bump into something. Fear had taken control.

Then I heard Nomaphelo whisper, "These people could be dangerous!"

As soon as she said that my knees became weak. Each step became an achievement. Nomaphelo lived in the area and probably knew who would be dangerous. If she was scared of those guys, I thought, then I should be scared as well, but the truth was that I was already shaking like a leaf.

I tried to calm myself down. If they hadn't harmed us earlier on, why would they harm us now? But I could hear the heavy breathing of Khaya and Bongani in front of me and knew that they were as scared as I was.

Nomaphelo put her small hand in mine and I held it tightly with the little strength that I still had. Her hand felt cold and she was trembling, but her shaky grip sent a message straight to my heart. I was her hope at that moment. I felt the connection between the two of us as our shivering fingers touched and suddenly I wished that we had walked in front, not at the back. Nomaphelo was the most vulnerable amongst us. It would be easy to attack us from behind.

I looked at her, trying to reassure her that everything would be all right, but I couldn't really see her face in the dark. If only I could have done something more, a touch was not enough, but I had never been in a situation where I had to protect someone when I was in the same danger. I held her hand and tried to be brave, but I was as scared as she was.

At that moment it became clear that the guys behind us were up to something. I heard their footsteps and it sounded like they were approaching fast. Now we were in trouble.

Having spent a long time in Cape Town I knew these guys would probably want to rob us of our cellphones and cash. We didn't have any valuable possessions with us, as we had left them at the flat, and I thought that the worst thing that could happen was that they would steal our clothes. I knew that some people had experienced such things in some parts of the Cape Flats, where gangsters would strip people naked and then let them go. I started to imagine myself running away naked towards town. All I hoped was that my friends wouldn't resist if these guys wanted to search us, as we are always told that one of the ways of dealing with criminals is to cooperate with them. We didn't have any money with us and I had never heard of a case where robbers attacked someone who didn't have any possessions and who didn't resist the robbery. Remember, they were five and we were four, they were all males and we were three men and one woman. They probably were hardened criminals, we were just plain law-abiding citizens. We were no match for them.

I was still weighing this up when Nomaphelo bumped against me again. In a state of shock I dropped her hand and for a moment I felt like I had betrayed her trust. The poor girl was as scared as a frog being faced by a snake.

The footsteps were still following us and they sounded closer than earlier. I saw Bongani looking back over his shoulder as if he suspected something. When I saw this I was also tempted to look behind me, but decided against it as by this time we were walking fast, bumping into one another, and I needed to concentrate on the path.

Then, as if we had some kind of telepathic communication, we all started running at the same time. Because there was no other way to run we all followed each other, running in the same direction, towards the big factory buildings. Running like this you would never know what had happened to the person behind you. What made things even scarier was that Nomaphelo, the girl, was the one behind me and I couldn't hear her footsteps. I thought of all the horror stories that I had heard. What if these thugs raped and killed her? I had read stories of people who raped women before killing them. Sometimes the robbers mutilated people and cut their private parts. The thought of her being in trouble was what made me look behind me to see if she was still safe. I feared more for her than for any of us.

I looked behind and I saw what I had never imagined. There they were, those five guys, all with guns in their hands.

One gun seemed to be shining brightly. I am not sure if it was my imagination but this one particular gun seemed to look gold. Again, my eyes reached for the guy with the maroon T-shirt and khaki pants. This time I noticed that he was also wearing a khaki sporty cap. Now it was obvious that these guys were really planning to do something to us, something bad and evil, and were not about to stop for any reason.

The first time I had touched a gun had been a few years ago. My father had just returned from Cape Town. Knowing that he was about to come home permanently and that crime – mainly theft – was starting to become more widespread, he had decided to get himself a gun. One day, not long after he had come home, he asked me to test it with him. We went out and found a place in the veld where no-one could see us. He handed it to me loaded, but as soon as I touched it I started shivering and nearly dropped it. I had never expected it to be so heavy.

My dad was enjoying himself, seeing a loudmouth like myself so afraid. I had always told him that I wasn't frightened of anything, but there I was, scared as a wet chicken. He took the gun away from me and fired a shot into the air. The sound was so loud that I nearly collapsed from shock.

That had been my one and only encounter with a gun and I had been nervous of them ever since.

Click, grrr, click, click, click. The weapons were being readied, now there was no doubting their intentions. They had all cocked their guns at the same time, with the precision of military men. Nomaphelo had started to cry openly from behind me and, as we ran, we all joined in, pleading with the guys not to harm us. As we began to plead with them so they started to shout obscenities at us. I had expected someone to say something like "Surrender all your possessions!", or "Put your hands up above your head!", but it was "Voetsek, motherfuckers!", "Fuck you dirty bastards!" all the way. We staggered forward hoping that they would spare us, pleading with them as we ran. Fear overcame me. I had already betrayed Nomaphelo by letting go of her hand. I knew that today would be my time; it would be my face and my story that would jump out of the newspaper. What many South Africans had already experienced was becoming my reality.

As I ran I prayed that someone would appear and disrupt them. If only the police would arrive or the security guards from the factories would hear them swearing at us and come to our rescue. I even wished that a train would appear and scare the thugs. But none of these things happened and I had only run about ten more steps when I heard the loudest sound, a sound like thunder. It was so loud that my eardrums felt like they had been burst open. It was so thunderous that it kept reverberating in my stomach long after it had sounded. A shot had been fired.

This brought my mind back to the sound my father's gun made when we were testing it out in the veld. My father's gun was like the snap of my fingers in comparison. This was the sound that the thunder from home makes during summer before a storm.

Fortunately for me, the bullet didn't catch me, but what about the others? In the dark I couldn't keep track of them. What if one of us was dead already? I wished I was dreaming and someone would just shake me, wake me up and tell me it was all a dream, but that was not to be. I wasn't dreaming. I wasn't hallucinating. I was wide awake in the real world. My knees became so weak I didn't know what to do. I felt like someone who had been running for a couple of kilometres, not just a few metres, but there were only two options, continue running or wait for a bullet to catch me.

I looked back and saw what looked like Nomaphelo right behind me. I tried to grab her hand again and run along with her, but this didn't help either of us and while we lost time trying to help each other along they kept on shooting at us. I wished I could do something for her, but there was absolutely nothing I could do, we were all going to die. We were just running so that we would die closer to the place where we stayed. At least that was the way it seemed to me.

At the same time they were still swearing at us: "Voetsek, voetsek, misunu yoonyoko, minqundu yoonyoko."

They were swearing at us about our mothers, the way gangsters would swear at a rival gang, the most disrespectful way of swearing at a person.

Then, somehow, I had managed to outrun Nomaphelo and Bongani and only Khaya was still ahead of me. Being new to Germiston I didn't know if I was running in the right direction. The big buildings in front of us seemed to be moving further and further away while all the time gunshots were sounding behind us. I don't know which was louder, the sound of my footsteps or the thudding of my heartbeat.

Still the gunshots kept sounding behind us and the criminals' voices continued to shout abuse. Their voices sounded as if they were just behind me. It was clear that they were keeping up the chase and I didn't know what had happened to my friends behind me. My heart was pumping even faster and louder by then. I can still remember jumping over the railway tracks. Even though each of the railway tracks was less than a metre wide it felt as if I was crossing an overflowing river hundreds of metres wide. By now I was sure my friends behind me were already dead and I was next.

I think I had barely left the railway lines when I heard a loud gunshot and felt something very hot pierce my back. At the same time I tripped on a rock and lost my balance. It all happened so fast that I didn't even notice that I was falling. I would have stretched my hands forward so that I didn't fall badly, but my hands were still in the sprinting position. I fell face first and only recognised that I was falling when I hit the ground.

Usually, when you fall, you try to get up, but I didn't. The last thing I heard was a cry that sounded like a dying person, the sound that actors make in movies before they fall down and die. After that I must have lost consciousness.

When I came round I thought I saw Bongani run past, crying as if he was hurt already. After that I heard some footsteps that I presumed belonged to Nomaphelo, but I couldn't see a thing. Then I lost consciousness for a second time.

When I opened my eyes again I felt a stinging pain in my lower abdomen and I knew I had been shot. There was this deafening noise in the atmosphere that sounded like that of a tractor and the ground seemed to be vibrating. I could see what looked like two poles right in front of my eyes and for a moment I thought they might be two of the poles from the fence that surrounded the railway lines, but I quickly realised that they were actually the legs of a person. There was someone standing right above my head. I thought it was one of my friends: Bongani or Khaya. I reached out so that I could support myself, but instead of helping me, the guy kicked me in my forehead and started shouting obscenities.

I tried to get up on my own, but my knees and my arms were weak and there was this stinging pain in my lower back from the bullet. Whenever I tried to get up the pain of the wound would drag me down. This didn't stop me though. I kept telling myself that I had to get up and face this monster. I wanted to look this man straight in the eye. I had this belief that when he saw how harmless a person I was, he would spare my life.

Eventually I gained enough strength to stand on my two legs. This time, he didn't kick me or insult me. Maybe, I thought, he had realised that I wasn't the person that he wanted to kill. But then I lifted my head and saw the horror!

It's not over yet

Right in front of me was the guy with the khaki cap. The guy looked me straight in the eyes and shouted, "Msunu kanyoko, ziphi kaloku eziny'izinja?"

It was at that moment I knew that there was no way I could survive. I had thought that if I looked him straight in the eye he would realise how big a mistake he had made. I believed that no-one would shoot someone that they didn't know, that he would recognise that I wasn't the person he was looking for and let me go, but when I looked up I saw that I was staring death in the eye. I saw danger, anger, stupidity, arrogance, evil, cruelty and merci-lessness. I was, I realised, seeing the devil.

The light from the lamppost shone off the barrel of the gun he was pointing at me. The gun was at less than an arm's length, probably a mere thirty centimetres, away from my chest. He was clearly becoming angrier – I still hadn't answered his first question – and he shouted, "Ufun'ukwenzani, mnqundu kanyoko?"

I tried to move my trembling lips to answer him, to tell him that I wasn't the person he thought I was, to beg for my life to be spared. But, alas, the words wouldn't come out of my mouth. All I could do was tremble. The only sound was my breath and my heartbeat.

Seeing that I wasn't answering him, he began to recite something that I couldn't understand. I think it must have been prison jargon because some of the words sounded a little familiar, but I couldn't understand what he meant. I have heard people who have spent some time in jail speaking prison language, but they are never clear when they speak it and I have never understood any of it. He kept reciting the same phrases and making gestures with his hands that I also didn't understand, but something still told me that he would forgive me if I tried to explain to him that I was not a threat to him in any way. I was convinced that he had mistaken me for his enemy. If I could only persuade him that I was only an innocent person who would never harm anyone, I was sure he would help me. I wasn't a local. I came from Cape Town. He would help me if he knew that I wasn't from around there, but when I opened my mouth to speak my throat was as dry as tree bark.

By that time the hand that was holding the gun had begun shaking vigorously as if the gun was becoming too heavy for him. I began to think that maybe I could try and grab it and point it back at him, but at that moment he clenched his left fist and I could see from the way he grinned that my time was up. Before I could even move my lips to cry out I heard a thundering bang and fell to the ground.

It felt as if I had been shot twice. It felt as if someone was pressing burning metal into my chest and back; grilling my flesh, the heat going right through me. There was no more time to speak and beg for my life to be spared, I was dead already.

I only realised I was still alive when he kicked me in the testicles and swore at me one more time in his, by then, hoarse voice. Then, again, loud thunder sounded, but I couldn't see the gun or the guy, all I could see were sparks, that looked like the stars, in front of my eyes.

He was busy muttering at me. From the words that he was us-
ing I noticed for the first time that he spoke my mother tongue –
isiXhosa. Imagine! During my stay in Germiston I had met very
few people who spoke my language with the proper accent. Now,
for the first time in my stay, I heard it spoken properly and the
man speaking it was the man hurling insults at me, the man killing
me with a gun. And not only was he killing me, he seemed determined to make sure that I experienced as slow and as painful a
death as possible. He wasn't just killing me, he was torturing me.

I was brought back to my own reality by a kick to the head and
another gunshot. The bullet probably missed me because I didn't
feel it hit me, but by then I didn't even know which part of my
body was injured and which was not. All that I knew was that I
was dying a very slow and very, very painful death. The blood was
streaming out of me like water out of a burst pipe.

It was at this point that I started to wish that I would die quickly. My prayers had changed. I no longer wished my life would be
spared. All I was asking God to do was to let me die. Dying had
to be better than what I was going through. I started to wish that
he would just shoot me in the head, but the guy wasn't in any
hurry, he wanted to make sure that I felt pain.

I heard another bang that shook my whole body and made me
think that my prayers for a quick death had finally been answered.
He had fired a shot straight through my belly and I could feel something very hot moving around inside my stomach. I didn't feel
much pain until he kicked me in the head. When he kicked me I
didn't only feel pain in my head but all my wounds felt as if something was forcing its way out of them. All that I could do was gasp.

The scariest thing was that I never seemed to lose consciousness. Instead, I was conscious for each and every second of it. I tried to pretend I was dead already, but the pain kept giving me away.

Finally, thinking I had to be dead, he dragged me onto the railway lines, muttering some more abuse. As he dragged me, I had to loosen up my body so that he didn't notice that I was still alive. I couldn't feel anything for a while until he put me down on top of the railway tracks and pushed my head against one of them.

The railway lines were very cold because of the weather and they made the pain worse, in particular the wound in my chest. The wound in my back felt as if a red-hot rod had been forced through it.

I heard a clicking sound and knew that he had pulled out his gun one more time and was pointing it at me. I was lying with my face down, so I couldn't see which part of my body he was targeting. He fired the fifth shot, which went through the left-hand side of my lower abdomen. I heard something drop onto the stones that you find underneath the railway tracks. It was the bullet. The bullet had exited my body just above the bladder area.

"Ifile le nja ngoku," he said, as he kicked me in the ribs one last time.

Railway lines

He turned away from me and took the first step towards the township. From the corner of my eye I could see him walking confidently towards the settlement. I was sure he was the same guy that I had noticed among that group, the one with the maroon T-shirt. It was clear that the reason I was so scared of him was simply that God was telling me that he was the one who would kill me.

After he crossed the railway lines I saw him tucking his gun into his pants. He looked behind once, perhaps to admire his handiwork, and then vanished into the settlement.

The strange thing was that I felt more despair than hope as I saw him disappear. He was the only person around, so if anyone was going to help me it would have to have been him. It was senseless, but I still harboured this idea that something would change his mind and he would come back and help me.

Finally I told myself that I was becoming stupid in my desperation. There was no way I could get help from anyone. I shifted back to reality again.

My teeth were covered with sand and the stones underneath the railway lines poked at my wounds even though I wasn't moving. All my muscles felt tense and painful and every breath I took made it feel like thorns were coming in through my nose and being pulled out through my wounds. My tongue stuck out of my mouth onto the rails and tears were flowing down my cheeks. The saliva was just pouring out of my mouth. I had no control over anything that was happening to me. I think I must have really looked like a dead dog.

I wanted to try and get up, but my whole body felt so numb and I couldn't feel my legs. My first attempt was to try and move my fingers. My left hand did respond, but my right hand wouldn't move. Next I tried to move my head. My neck was stiff but I was able to lift my head. As I did, I noticed that there was a bridge above me. Whenever I opened my eyes I saw double and it looked to me as if the bridge was moving around me, but I could hear the cars passing above me. I tried to listen for footsteps in case someone who could help me was walking on the bridge, but the sound of the gunshots kept reverberating in my ears and I couldn't hear anything of the sort.

At this moment, I started to think about all the things that I had done in my short life. I knew that there was no turning back. I was dying. And, one by one, all the people that I might have hurt in my life, the people that I had never apologised to, started flashing before my eyes.

The first person that I thought about was my dear mother. My mother is a very quiet person who doesn't like to raise her voice. I thought about all the things that might have hurt her: stealing her sugar when I was young, letting the livestock go astray when I was in my preteens because I spent time playing with friends, not telling her how I loved her in my adulthood, coming home drunk and just about anything and everything else you could think of.

Then I thought of the way I used to not follow my father's orders, the way I laughed when he told me to go to church. As you know, my father was a well-respected preacher in his beloved United Methodist Church of Southern Africa. I could remember how churchgoers used to tell me what a good preacher he was. I have a very strong resemblance to my father so everyone kept saying that I would grow to be a great preacher like him, but I had never had a relationship with God. I started thinking about numerous preachers who had preached about God to me but I, being the hip guy that I was, had never set my foot in any church, except for the night services.

There I was, dying like a stray dog. I knew that my name would be forgotten and I would go straight to hell. I wished I could turn back the clock and undo all the wrongs that I had done in the past. I had let myself and my family down.

Somewhere, lost in these thoughts, I must have passed out, because the next thing I remember was hearing the sound of a hooter. Somehow I had forgotten that I was on a railway line and that a train could come at any time. When I regained consciousness the initial feeling was that of relief. The parts of my body I could feel were agony, but I knew that the train would finish with all my pain, the train would end my misery in an instant.

I was wearing a green jacket and black tracksuit pants, which I knew would make it difficult for the train driver to see me. I also knew that even if he did see me there was no way that he would be able to stop the train in time because a train takes something like two hundred metres to come to a halt. All I had to do was lie there.

The hooter continued to sound and it was getting closer. When I lifted my head I saw the yellow light of an oncoming train. The train was hooting continuously. Clearly the driver had seen me on the tracks despite my dark clothing.

I wanted to keep lying there so that the train could just smash me once and for all and relieve me of the agony, but the driver had seen me and I suddenly recalled the documentary I had seen on the television about the trauma that train drivers go through when someone commits suicide on the train tracks. I remember one train driver, a grown man, weeping openly about the pain he goes through every time the train that he is driving kills someone.

Once I had thought about the driver I began to think about my family. If I kept lying on the railway tracks the train would smash me into an unrecognisable paste. This would make it difficult to identify me and they would have to bury some flesh unsure if it really was mine. With my friends dead no-one would know who was who among the corpses. For all I knew, they too had been shot down and put on the railway tracks.

I wanted my family to be able to identify my body and bury it in the way that they wanted. If I didn't have an honourable death at least I should have a dignified burial.

I decided to try and roll over the rails onto the stones, but there was a problem with trying to roll away from the tracks: I didn't know which side to move to in order to escape the train. By this time, the train was about fifty metres away so I could see it clearly, but I still couldn't tell which set of tracks it was on. I was scared of moving, only to find I had actually rolled onto the tracks of the oncoming train, thereby getting myself smashed by the same train I had thought I was escaping from. In the end I just decided to roll over to my right-hand side.

A split second after rolling away from the railway tracks, I saw the train passing just centimetres away from my body. I was so close that all I could see were the wheels. The wind from under the train was suffocating; it was thick, cold and smelt of oil.

The train seemed to take forever to pass me, because with each passing wheel, the ground shook and it felt as if I was being sucked towards the train.

After what seemed like a full hour the train had passed completely. I lifted my head up and saw a large pool of blood. The blood was splashed all over the place. It looked like two people had been shot. There was just no way that all this blood could have come out of one person, and there was definitely no way that that person was still alive.

I let my head fall back onto the stones asking myself what I ever did to deserve such pain and agony. Was God there? Did He see what was happening? Why didn't He do anything to stop those thugs from committing such an atrocity? Where was He when I needed Him the most?

The journey

I eventually decided to stop blaming God and get closer to the main road so that people would see and help me. After all, God was still by my side, because I was still alive.

I tried to get up but my whole lower body didn't want to move, my legs were numb. My second attempt was more successful, I was able to lift my whole body up, but I was frightened when I saw how much blood there was on the T-shirt and the jacket that I was wearing. My clothing was soaked in blood.

The main road was approximately three hundred metres away. Having managed to stand I staggered towards it, hoping someone would appear and help me or call an ambulance.

Each and every single step that I took was an effort because every step seemed to aggravate my wounds. It was especially bad when I moved my right leg. Just to lift the leg was an effort. I would first have to tighten my bullet-riddled tummy before taking a step. The pain became more intense with every step.

Breathing was another effort. Every time I inhaled or exhaled, blood would come out of my wounds and because of this I would try to withhold my breath for five or six steps so that there wouldn't be too much air going in and out through my wounds. Unfortunately the problem would come back as soon I had to resume breathing.

I might have staggered about ten metres when I felt something

45

moving up and down inside my stomach. It was a bullet and it was so hot that I began to groan in pain. Every step I took caused more painful movement inside my belly.

This is the moment that I really began to fight for my life. I had rolled over to avoid the train because I had wanted my family to be able to identify my body and bury it the way they wanted, but now I thought about how God had spared my life and asked myself why He would do that only to let me die. If I had been shot so many times, survived the train and walked such a long distance, I had to live. All of that could not be in vain. A quick death was not an option, a dignified death was not good enough, only life would do.

God had delivered me and shown me a path. I knew at that moment that He had plans for me. God had brought me onto this earth to conquer and there was no way I would let the devil have the last say. I wanted to live to see what God had in store for me.

As I fought the pain from my wounds I remembered a line from a gospel song that went something like "I don't believe He got me this far to leave me". I prayed hard, with tears streaming down my cheeks, for God to continue the job that He had already started – to save me.

I staggered on.

After I had covered a little distance I saw something that looked like a person and I was overcome with mixed emotions. Was this the person who would save my life or was it one of the thugs coming back to finish me off? I stopped moving, but there was no way I could hide. I hadn't seen the rest of the thugs since the attack began and I was sure that they were chasing my friends, which meant that they could come back and finish me off at any moment.

After waiting for what felt like an eternity I realised that this wasn't a person. A person would have called out to me or moved. When I got closer this "person" turned out, fortunately or unfortunately, to be an electric pole.

I think I was about ten metres away from the main road when my legs gave in. I fell down right there and the tears flowed as I knelt, helpless, on the ground. I knew that no-one was going to come and pick me up and take me to the main road for the motorists to see and I knew that my legs wouldn't carry me any more, but despite this I told myself that I wasn't going to die. I told myself that I was going to get to the main road and I was going to get help. I told myself that I was going to beat all the odds and survive, paralysed or not. The only question was how I was going to get there.

Eventually I decided that the only way to get to the main road was to crawl until I reached it. I had to get to the road.

I thought of my family and visualised the pain they would feel if I couldn't find the strength to make it to the road and I decided to face the fire and drag myself to survival.

After crawling painfully across the waste ground I finally managed to get to the edge of the pavement. By now my T-shirt was so blood-soaked that you could see the bullet wounds through it.

Initially, I managed to stand , waving and screaming hysterically at the oncoming traffic, hoping that a motorist would stop, or at least call someone who would come and help. But no-one stopped. The motorists seemed not to care about this wounded, bloodied individual by the side of the road. I guess being a young black male didn't help either. The motorists, my only source of help, looked at me with suspicion. People probably just saw me as a gangster. In their eyes I was someone who deserved it. If only I could have explained to them who I was and what had happened to me.

At this stage I started to lose my voice. All that I could manage to do was to wave my hand to the passing motorists. Still, nobody bothered to stop.

There was this particular brown Toyota van whose driver went beyond not helping me. The car left the middle of the lane and approached me as if to knock me dead. I didn't have enough energy to jump away from the road. All I could do was to let myself fall to the side of the road. I wasn't sure if I could even do that before the car made contact.

Miraculously I was able to fall and roll over, aggravating my wounds once more. After all the effort that I put into getting to the road you can imagine just how difficult it was going to be to get up from that fall. I coughed once again and groaned from the pain as blood streamed out of the two wounds in my belly.

As I lay there a bus, which I assumed came from the South West Mines hostel, approached. The bus was moving slowly, increasing the chances of the driver and the passengers noticing me. Again, I was wrong. The bus just passed, without even stopping. But, as the bus went past, I heard a man's voice calling for the driver to stop, but the driver ignored him. God bless that man, at least he tried.

Lying there on the side of the road, hopes diminishing, pain increasing, energy decreasing, breathing slowly, I composed a short prayer: "God save me, You have pulled me this far, You can't let me down now. I know with Your power I will make it."

The night had become even colder and my wounds were becoming ever more painful. The pain was excruciating. Seconds felt like hours, minutes felt like days, hours felt like years. After so much pain and suffering and courage and perseverance I began to be certain that all my efforts were going to be in vain. My body felt even weaker and my chances of survival seemed even slimmer. Even my tears had dried up.

I must have been there for about thirty minutes or more when I saw what looked like the shadows of three people on the other side of the road. They stood surrounding what appeared to be a sleeping person. I tried to scream aloud so that they would hear me, but my voice was gone.

I resorted to waving my left hand as my right hand wouldn't move. Finally one of those three gentlemen bent forward and put his hand against his forehead to see what was happening on the other side of the road. Luckily he saw me. I heard him shouting out to his friends in isiZulu, "Awu bafethu, naw'umuntu ngale komgwaqo!"

They all rushed to my side of the road and picked me up. As they carried me back across the road, they told me that one of my friends had been shot dead and was lying on the other side of the road. My mind started racing. Who would it be? Khaya?

I started shivering at the thought of it being Khaya. We'd come a long way together. I knew what it would mean to his family if he died. He was the breadwinner.

Second scenario: Bongani. Again this would be a very bitter

pill to swallow. After the death of his brother, less than a year before, his passing would be a devastating blow to everyone who knew him.

Third scenario: Nomaphelo. Once more this would be a tragedy. It's never good to lose someone so young, sweet and loving.

The worst part about all these scenarios was that these people would have been killed while they were in my company. I had failed all of them. I had failed their families.

The three men took me to the other side of the road and put me under a lamppost. It was only then that I saw the body of a middle-aged man. Both his hands were stretched out, an indication that he had been shot while he lifted his hands up in surrender. There was a bullet wound in his forehead.

Initially, I too thought he was one of my friends, but I later realised that he wasn't. In fact, I had never seen him before. But, I asked myself, if this man was killed in this manner, how on earth would my friends have survived? There was no way that they were still alive.

Waiting and waiting

One of the men called an ambulance from his cellphone and told me that it was on its way, but by that time even a single second felt like a full hour. Nothing and no-one could have comforted me and the fact that I had been put next to a corpse didn't help. I kept telling myself that I would join him soon.

At this time the pain was unbearable and I was beginning to hallucinate; seeing many people whose faces I knew, dead and alive. They formed a queue and resembled people who were viewing a corpse at a funeral.

I was awakened from these hallucinations by the loud sound of an ambulance siren. When I opened my eyes there were the blinding lights of a big ambulance. I was so badly injured that at first the paramedics thought that I was the dead one, but luckily the gentleman who had called the ambulance told them otherwise. They put me on a stretcher, helped me into the ambulance and put me on a drip.

I was tempted to ask one of the paramedics if I would make it, but when I opened my mouth to speak he simply told me to keep praying and not to think about dying. He also told me that I had to make sure that I didn't fall asleep, because if I closed my eyes it would be very difficult to wake up. To me all this meant that I was going to die. All that effort and I had only bought myself a little time in this world.

I wished they would put me to sleep as I wasn't breathing properly any more, I was simply gasping from the intensity of the pain, but when I asked for painkillers I was told that I was at a stage where I couldn't have any.

When I raised my head to look around I saw the dead man, his face turning from black to blue, his eyes wide open. The man was dead, free of all the pain that was still troubling me. He was in heaven.

Every time I tried to shift my imagination to something less traumatic, the pain would bring me back. The paramedic by my side kept on trying to reassure me that I would make it, but he didn't sound convinced and not for a single second did I believe him. They were busy on their two-way radios informing the hospital about the dying patient that they were bringing. As you know, I was that patient and I could hear every word.

I forced my voice out and asked the paramedics how far away the hospital was. The road felt so bumpy – even though it was a well-tarred city road – and the pain brought about by every bump was unbearable. The gentleman by my side told me that we were *only* twenty minutes away.

All this time I was still on that stretcher, attached to a drip. The paramedic would hold my hand and put his palm on my forehead to check my pulse from time to time. Because I had no-one with me who knew me, they had to ask me questions directly. Because of the pain and my injuries it would take me two or three minutes just to answer a simple question like "Where do you stay?"

They got confused when I told them that I was staying in Khaya's flat, which was called Pirrowville, but that I actually came from Cape Town. To them it sounded like I was saying that I stayed in Parow Valley in Cape Town. I think they thought I was losing consciousness so I had to omit the Cape Town part and just tell them where I stayed in Germiston.

After what felt like seven hours we arrived at Natalspruit Hospital. The paramedics lifted me out of the ambulance and carried me into the hospital. Inside the hospital some people, whose loved ones had no doubt just passed away or been badly injured, were crying out. I would have joined them, but by then I had lost my voice completely and all my tears had dried up. The paramedics handed some papers to the hospital staff, wished me well and left to save some other lives. Their job was done as far as my case was concerned. God bless them.

Lying in the hospital I waited for someone to come and help me. Every time I saw someone approaching I would wonder if they were the doctor. I was very afraid. Surely, I thought, the bullets inside my chest were doing more damage while I was lying there.

When they did finally come to help me, I was told that the doctor was still busy operating on another patient and would only be ready to operate on me in forty-five minutes. Then, instead of them picking me up and moving me to another bed, the nurses told me to roll over onto the bed near the one I was in. I thought this was a little insensitive considering my wounds, but I must admit that, aside from this, they were very nice to me.

They used scissors to cut my T-shirt off my body and took all my clothes away. It was at that moment that I finally realised how

53

bad my wounds were. There were bullet holes in my body. Horrible holes. There was this one wound, in particular, that had some flesh sticking out of it . . .

I think it was when they noticed how scared I was that they covered me with a white cloth. Even though the wounds were covered, whenever I inhaled, I could see the cloth sticking to my skin as if it was being sucked into them. When I exhaled some blood would come through the cloth. I had also seen that my pubic area was covered in blood, leading me to the fear that my genitalia had been affected. This thought was very scary. What if my sexual organs were destroyed? I began to imagine dying without ever fathering a child. I had always told myself that I never wanted to bring a child into this world. Now, suddenly, I was worried about not being able to be a father.

Then I started to think about even more horrific possibilities. I didn't know exactly how much damage the bullets had done to my body. I might be paralysed. I couldn't feel my legs at all and there was this particular bullet wound in my lower back that made it feel as if my whole waist area was just a hole. I was a scared man.

However, there was this one nurse who kept reassuring me that I would make it. She even prayed with me while we waited for the doctor to finish the operation that he was busy with. This angel of God didn't leave my side once. She kept trying to distract me from concentrating on my situation. She told me she didn't know why, but she really believed that I would make it, that God would see to it that I survived. God bless her.

I regained hope when this guy stepped into the room to assess me. He had dreadlocks and looked like a township pantsula, but he sounded very sincere. He told me that the doctor would finish in the next ten minutes. This gentleman turned out to be Dr Moagi, who was an assistant to Dr Gerard Karera, the doctor who was going to operate on me. My angel, the friendly nurse by my side, told me that I would recover because she knew these two doctors to be excellent at their work.

In the meantime I was made to sign a "consent form". Don't be confused by the inverted commas, I just don't believe that anyone in my condition wouldn't consent to being operated on if it meant that there was a chance of saving his or her life. I couldn't even write my name properly because of the pain. When I wrote in the wrong space the nurse who had brought the form sounded irritated and told me to write it again. I wept, but I did write it one more time, with my angel nurse supporting my arm.

Dr Moagi went inside the operating theatre and then quickly came out again. He instructed the nurses to take me to X-ray because Dr Karera was about to finish with the patient. By then there were three nurses by my side, each one of them with their own words of encouragement. Still, this one particular nurse seemed to outdo everyone, she sounded and acted as if she knew me personally.

After I had been X-rayed they pushed my bed into the operating theatre. I was injected with what I thought was something to put me to sleep, but the only thing that seemed to happen was that my vision became blurry. I thought I wouldn't feel any pain during the operation. How wrong I was. When they first cut through my lower abdomen it was like nothing I've ever felt before. The pain was so excruciating that I wanted to scream my lungs out. I felt like kicking one of them to show them that I could feel everything. I tried to move my lips, but they were numb. My jaw was stiff and my eyes felt cold.

I guess now that the medication was starting to kick in, but I could still hear some of the things they said to one another. I heard someone saying something that sounded like, "We're losing him!"

Then, later, I could feel something moving around in my stomach and, later still, I heard someone saying what sounded like "Not another one!"

It was at that moment that I finally dozed off. After this I don't know what happened, I had no thoughts, no dreams, nothing.

I'm back

I dreamt that I was surrounded by a great many people speaking different languages. In the dream I was wearing athletics gear and there was sweat all over my body. I was utterly exhausted and was lying down but, for some reason, there was a pillow under my head.

When I woke up I found myself surrounded by an army of people with their faces covered by white cloths. The light was too bright for my eyes and I had to close them again immediately.

When I forced myself to open my eyes again I noticed that all of the people were clad in green gowns, but I still didn't know where I was. It was scary to see people whose faces were covered except for their eyes but, luckily, no-one seemed to notice me as they were too busy chatting to one another.

I tried to listen to what they were saying and noticed that they were speaking mainly in Sesotho and English, not isiXhosa. It was at that moment that I began to think about where I was and why. Slowly, it dawned on me then that I was in Gauteng, not Cape Town. Then I began to remember everything that had happened and got so scared that I had to close my eyes again.

I started breathing faster and it was at that moment that one of the nurses noticed I was awake. She couldn't believe her eyes and shouted to her colleagues. Everybody was so overwhelmed that they almost unanimously called out: "Thembelani, are you awake?"

There were screams of "Ke mohlolo ntho ena!" and "Habe bantu uNkulunkulu mkhulu!" There was jubilation inside the ward.

Soon the doctor was called and moments later he rushed in. It seemed to me as if he must have just been in the corridor. Even the doctor couldn't believe it when he saw me with my eyes open.

Surely they had seen many people in my condition, I thought to myself, as the attention started to scare me. Maybe my recovery was somehow quicker than expected.

They tried to check if I was okay by asking me some questions. They asked me what my name was, whether I knew what had brought me to the hospital and what day it was.

I answered all their questions correctly except for what day of the week it was. I had been shot on the Wednesday so I thought that it was Thursday, the following day.

At that they all laughed and told me that it wasn't Thursday, but Sunday, and I had been in bed since Wednesday.

Four days in bed unconscious? I asked myself in disbelief.

Everybody gathered around me as if I came from Heaven. I looked at them all, trying to find a familiar face from the day I was admitted, but I didn't recognise any of them. My mind was racing back through the events at the hospital. I thought about the angel nurse who was by my side before the operation, but I couldn't remember what she looked like, let alone her name.

The doctor introduced himself to me as Dr Gerard Karera, the one who had operated on me. He also said he was going to invite his assistant, Dr Moagi, to come and meet me.

Once all the attention had died down I couldn't help noticing that there were pipes inserted into many parts of my body. To begin with there was a pipe that went in through my left nostril. I must tell you that this particular pipe didn't make breathing a comfortable activity. Every time I inhaled or exhaled it felt as if this pipe was piercing the flesh inside my nostril. It went down to my throat, which made it difficult when I had to swallow. As if that wasn't enough I felt the urge to swallow saliva almost every minute because of the pipe.

While I was busy examining the pipes in my body, the doctor and one of the nurses were busy working on the machines that I was attached to. Meanwhile the other medical staff kept coming into the ward one by one to have a look at me. It seemed as if everybody who entered noticed me and couldn't believe that I was really awake.

I also couldn't help noticing that in this particular ward there were only three patients. When I tried to turn my head so that I could see the other patients I quickly found that the numerous pipes attached to my body made it impossible. The nurse, seeing my frustration, quickly asked me not to move a lot as I would aggravate my wounds.

I began to think about my friends. What would I do if they were really dead? How would I inform their families of their death? I closed my eyes every time I thought of Khaya and Bongani and Nomaphelo.

All this time the doctor was busy jotting down something in my folder, which I presumed were instructions to the nurses on how to take care of me. When he had finished writing he told me not to try and get out of the bed as I was still in a bad condition and to call the nurses every time I felt anything strange.

At that moment I must admit that I wasn't feeling any pain. All I could feel was a numbness. Apart from the numbness I just felt tired, like I had just run the Comrades Marathon.

After the doctor left I started to do my own thorough examination. Seeing that I was able to breathe, see and hear, I became worried about my ability to walk. Would I ever be able to use all my limbs? I tried to move my legs, and guess what? I could move them. I let out a big sigh of relief: "Thank you, God, for this."

There was a catheter attached to the lower left part of my abdomen that contained a liquid that looked like bile. This really scared me to death. Also, when I looked down my chest, I noticed that there was long band of bandage that stretched down to the bladder area. This bandage also extended sideways across my chest area to form a cross. My heart was covered with a wide bandage as well. I could see some bloodstains on the bandages and I could smell strong ointment.

So, there I was, all covered in bandages with pipes inserted in all the holes in my body, some pipes attached to a monitor that looked like a television, an oxygen mask covering my face and two electrodes on either side of my chest.

There was also a pipe that was inserted in my penis. This apparently was the urinary catheter. The pipe went down the whole length of my penis and was attached to a transparent plastic bag that was half-full of urine. I could also see the droplets of urine sliding down the pipe into the bag. This, too, didn't feel comfortable at all. If I couldn't even urinate by myself, then I must be helpless, I thought.

The bed was well adjusted so that I was comfortable, but every time I breathed in my body felt as if I was standing upside down. The mask that they had covered my face with didn't help matters as every time I exhaled it would make an irritating sound. There was this machine sound that kept groaning by my bedside and at times my vision would be so blurry it was as if I was looking through a sheet of water.

The nurse would ask me from time to time if I was comfortable. At this stage I was only left with three nurses, the rest had left for their respective wards, I assumed. One of these nurses was Sister Connie, the one who spent time by my side when I was admitted, my angel. She seemed to be the happiest of them all. To her, my wellbeing was a personal thing, she was so dedicated. Was she real or was she an angel sent from God? I would ask myself from time to time when I saw her smile and heard her comforting words.

Even when the other nurses were dressing my wounds or cleaning me up, she would monitor them closely and make sure that I didn't get hurt in the process. She always gave me her reassuring smile when I was suffering and it made everything feel a little better.

I would drop a tear every once in a while because of the gratitude I felt for the hospital staff, especially Sister Connie.

From time to time I would turn my head a little to look at the other severely injured patients around me and see the pain and agony written all over their faces. Their eyes told their stories. However, the way they looked at me showed that they were all feeling sorry for me.

On my left-hand side there was a man, Sipho, who had been

involved in a terrible car accident. One of the nurses told me that he had arrived during the night. The nurses would talk to him as if he was conscious and reassure him that he would be fine, but, the way he looked, you would have sworn he was already dead.

There was an elderly woman by his side, praying. This lady, between her prayers, would look at me and the other patients and weep. She was the only visitor allowed in the ward outside of visiting hours. All that she did, besides praying, was to clasp the patient's hand, but the guy was motionless and emotionless.

After a while I decided to stop looking at Sipho because the more I looked at him the worse I felt. The nurses had told me that I had been in a worse state than Sipho when I had come to the ward and, if it was true, I had a lot to worry about. In fact, so pitiful was my life at that moment that everyone who entered the ward seemed to look at me and look away as if they didn't want to see a dying man.

I felt so helpless. I was covered with sweat and every breath that I took was a big effort. I closed my tired eyes, shed a tear or two, prayed and thanked God for sparing my life.

The visitors

Not long after I had woken up, a nurse came to my bedside and told me that I had some visitors and asked me if I was ready to talk to them. Of course I was. I nodded my head, smiled and signalled for her to let them in. What better way to prove to yourself that you really are alive than to see the people that you know and love talking to? I felt as if I had been dead for a very long time. I was burning with anticipation.

The blue door swung open and a hand appeared. They came in reluctantly, one by one, not knowing what to expect. I could see them out of the corner of my eye. Surely my condition was worse than even I thought it was if it needed this much courage just to come and see me.

First in was Khaya, who looked at me once and began smiling from ear to ear. "Oh God, he is alive," I muttered, relieved of my worst fear.

Next to come into the ward was Siya, a short, stocky character who stayed in Midrand. We had spoken on my arrival in Jozi and had planned to meet at his place one weekend before I left for Cape Town. Little had we known that we would meet like this. I had known Siya for eight years and I had never seen him get emotional over anything, but today was different, it was all he could do to stop the tears from falling.

The nurse removed the oxygen mask from my face so that I

63

would be able to talk freely. Siya has a very good sense of humour, but on that day it was all gone. He was cautious about everything he said and did. Both he and Khaya seemed to have been told that I would be very sensitive and they just didn't know what to do or say. Being the tough nut that I am I broke the ice, as I usually do. I made a good observation about how ugly Khaya looked when he was sad. That was it, the ice was broken and they were just themselves after that, which was exactly what I wanted.

We were still chatting when my two other friends, Siviwe and Bongani, came into the ward. The puzzle was almost complete, there was just one final piece missing.

"Where is Nomaphelo, is she alive?" I asked.

I tried to examine their faces as the atmosphere became tense again. Khaya tried to say something, but seemed to choke on the words and in the end all he could do was point at Bongani.

"What did they do to her?" I asked.

All of a sudden my heart started pounding faster as I imagined what might have happened to the poor girl. Did they rape and kill her?

Finally Bongani covered his face with his hand and answered, "She is alive. A hospital counsellor from East London called us on her behalf. She was admitted for shock and had been advised to call us and talk to us as part of her healing. She is in a bad state but, physically, no harm was done to her."

When I heard of her survival I started smiling with relief and tears started streaming down my face. The nurse in attendance came closer when she noticed the situation and asked me if I was okay.

"I couldn't be better," I said between gasps and tears. She gave a reassuring smile and left us to continue with our conversation.

I felt huge relief to find out all of them were alive, but Bongani looked sad. He obviously felt sorry for me, but he was, no doubt, also thanking God that he wasn't the one lying on that hospital bed. It was clearly not easy for him to see me in the state I was in and I'm sure he was also thinking about his brother who had been stabbed to death.

As for my other friend, Siviwe, he was literally shaking. He was trying to look strong but it was all just too much for him.

They told me that Khaya's younger brother, Khanyisa, was sitting outside as he couldn't bring himself to even enter the ward.

Khanyisa knew me as this hyperactive, strong man who was always joking and never seemed to be bothered by anything, so it would be very difficult to see me in such a state. I asked Bongani to call him in and to tell him that I was fine and that he needn't be scared. After a few moments he came in reluctantly, his hands behind his back, shaking. He greeted me in a stuttering voice, but I could see he was relieved to see me talking and smiling.

He didn't spend much time in the ward though, and after we had been talking for a little while he left in a hurry. This was after I told him not to worry about my condition and to continue doing the good things that he did: to work hard at school and be a good man. Apparently, I was later told by Khaya, Khanyisa believed that these are the things people say unintentionally before they pass on. At that moment he thought I was going to die.

Never before did I admire flowers like I did that day. To me flowers were always for women, but on that day it was different.

Siya had picked one stem in the hospital garden for me. When I looked at it, it wasn't just a flower, it represented the importance of life. It represented the way Siya cared about me as a person and a friend. A simple flower that day just took on a different meaning. I know the people who know me would probably say that this is very unThembelani-like, but I smelled that flower and marvelled at its scent.

From time to time I looked around to check if all my friends were still in the room. I looked into the eyes of each person, to give them my individual attention, and they looked back. I closed my eyes and the tears flowed. My friends had brought some tissues with them and, because I couldn't wipe my own tears away, they helped me. Everything that they said and did felt so special to me, I felt blessed to have caring friends like those around me.

It was then that they told me about their previous visits to the hospital. I didn't remember any of these as I was unconscious the whole time. I didn't remember seeing anyone prior to the Sunday when I woke up.

One day when they came, they told me, they were with Isaac and Justice, my other friends that I had known since our days at varsity, good friends indeed. Apparently Isaac couldn't get himself close to me as he said that I was in the worst shape that a person could be in. On their first visit my whole body was so bloated that I was unrecognisable. None of them believed the doctors when they said I was alive. They told me that I could open my eyes, but that I didn't recognise anyone except for Khaya.

After we had talked about their previous visits I asked them about what had really happened after I had been shot.

Khaya told me that as soon as the first shot sounded, everybody ran in the same direction. I remembered well that we all kept bumping into one another, all of us screaming, none of us knowing if one of us had been shot already. Each one of us just waiting for a bullet to strike.

Bongani remembered seeing me fall and both he and Khaya remembered my scream as I went down. It was my own scream that I had heard as I fell. Bongani had tripped over my legs as he passed, but he couldn't remember seeing Nomaphelo, although I was sure I had heard her footsteps nearby.

Khaya had continued to run towards the factories that we had been heading for all along. Eventually he ran into a group of security guards, the same ones who I had hoped would come and rescue me, but they mistook him for a thug and pointed their guns at him. They had heard the gunshots and probably thought he was a robber. At first they had tried to beat him up, but it soon became obvious to them that he wasn't a criminal and, after searching him, they let him go. When they let him go, he had continued to run until he got into the flat, where he threw himself on his bed and began to cry uncontrollably.

Bongani had run in the wrong direction, confused by the gunshots behind him. He had heard some screams but was unable to tell who they belonged to. He remembered falling down as he crossed the road and almost getting hit by a speeding car. When he'd looked around he discovered that he was running in the opposite direction from the flat. He turned around and had arrived at the flat sometime after the traumatised Khaya.

It is only when they both got into the flat that they realised that

Nomaphelo and I were nowhere to be found. Apparently they had initially hoped that we had gone to seek refuge at the police station. Then it started to dawn on them that we had probably been shot dead. They had gone to Germiston police station to report the matter, but they couldn't wait for the police van and went back to the flat to tell the neighbours what had happened. They quickly formed a search party and went looking for the two of us, but when they got to the place where I had fallen all that they could see was a pool of blood.

Khaya and Bongani told me that they gave up searching for us after several hours and went to sleep with the intention of looking for us the following morning. The following day they finally located me at the Natalspruit Hospital in Katlehong.

The hardest part, Khaya told me, was not knowing how to inform my parents about the incident. They couldn't decide who would tell my parents, what to say or how to say it. Khaya and Siya were the ones who finally called my father and broke the news. They said that my mother nearly collapsed when she heard what had happened.

My friends kept visiting me in the hospital but I was unconscious most of the time and, even when I seemed awake, I didn't recognise them. The hospital staff had allowed them to visit outside normal visiting hours as they were my only family, the only people who knew me. Yes, everybody had already given up hope, they all thought I wouldn't make it. They kept coming in every day to check on my progress but, until Sunday morning, they had never dared to hope that I might recover.

As for Nomaphelo, they later heard that she had climbed over the gates into one of the nearby factories, where the security guards offered her shelter. She had been so traumatised that she couldn't even speak, all she could do was point and sob. Fortunately, thanks be to God, she was unharmed.

She stayed at the factory for the entire night and asked the security guards to escort her home the following morning. She packed her bags the very same day and made her way back to East London, vowing never to return to Johannesburg.

But even in East London the poor girl was too traumatised to leave her home. And, eventually, the trauma had overpowered her. She collapsed and was admitted to hospital.

Khaya told me that she had called my number every day to monitor my situation. Khaya and Bongani had kept my cellphone with them at all times and she was one of the most frequent callers, but she was not the only one. Khaya and Bongani slowly told me about all the callers: family, colleagues from Cape Town and even strangers who had heard my story.

That Sunday was a very special day to me; I wished it would never end, that my friends would stay there until I got discharged from the hospital. But, eventually, a nurse came and signalled to the guys that their time was up. My friends wished me well and left, promising to come again the following day.

Alone again

When I woke up again it was night-time. Initially I was surprised to see that my friends were no longer with me. The lights were on and the machines were still making their constant, annoying sounds. When the people spoke, they spoke very softly so as not to disturb the patients. The atmosphere was sombre.

As there was no-one fussing over me, I took the opportunity to roll my eyes around and check on the other patients. The two patients on either side of me looked unconscious and the nurses had gathered around one patient on my far right, whom I didn't remember being in the ward before. What I did notice, though, was that I felt a little more energetic than before I had slept. The visit from my friends and the news about Nomaphelo had made me even stronger. I was feeling more alive. I appreciated all the company and encouragement that the nursing staff had given me, but it was a little different. They had to divide their attention between me and the other patients. It was nice to have my own visitors who had come specifically to see me. They were the closest thing I had to family.

As I lay there thinking back over the visit I tried to ignore the pain, but I was in some discomfort. The sweat kept pouring down my face despite the fact that the room temperature was quite normal. The pipe that went up through my nose and down my throat was still in place and every time I swallowed my throat hurt.

Coughing was also a problem. When I coughed I would feel pain in my chest, my abdomen and my back. It felt as if my body was cut in half. I would be scared whenever I felt an urge to cough. I didn't know if my belly was cut open underneath those bandages and the thought that it might be worried me a lot.

The memory of my ordeal had been stirred up by Khaya and Bongani and I spent the entire evening asking myself whether it was possible to survive such an ordeal. Could I really live through such a thing? And then I began to ask more difficult questions. If I survived would I ever be able to walk properly again? Would I ever be able to get married and have children? Who would take care of me if I needed special attention? Would my family be supportive enough? How would my girlfriend react? How would I survive?

And then, finally, I started to ask myself the question that would always be at the back of my mind: Why was I shot in the first place?

These questions kept me awake for the better part of the night. I would sob heavily every time I thought of my mother and the pain that she must be feeling but, eventually, around midnight, I fell asleep.

During my sleep I dreamed I was at home, in Engcobo, playing around with my family, laughing out loud. In that dream, my father kept shaking my hand as if to congratulate me on something I had done. I don't know why my father always featured prominently in my dreams while I was in hospital because, whenever I was awake, it was my mother that I always thought about. I was very worried about how this tragedy might have affected her, especially considering her high blood pressure.

You know, when you are in a condition like I was, you sometimes forget about you, the person who is directly involved in such a situation; instead, you keep wondering about your loved ones. The same goes for your fellow patients. You tend to worry about them more than you worry about yourself. I found this to be an escape mechanism. Whenever I felt an urge for self-pity, I would look around at the other patients.

I woke the following morning at about six to realise that I was still in the intensive care unit. Half-asleep and having forgotten that I couldn't move I thought I could just get up and go to the toilet. But I couldn't seem to move any part of my body and, opening my eyes, I instantly remembered where I was and, the seriousness of my condition. I was still dependent on the machines and I didn't know how long it would take or whether I would ever get up and walk properly again.

I think that being in the ICU is one of the most hopeless scenarios one can ever imagine. You just know that you are only one step from dying. Very few people get out of the ICU alive. Whenever I remembered where I was, I knew that I was one of those whose death wouldn't come as a shock. In our communities once you hear that somebody is in the ICU, you immediately condition yourself for the devastating news of their death; my case would not be an exception.

When the nurses did their daily prayer sessions in the ward I would just close my eyes and cry. The prayers were supposed to give us hope, but when someone prays for your life you can't help feeling that it is about to end.

However, there were other days when I felt more at home in

the ICU. For example, one day the nurses were playing music on a small radio, perhaps to take their minds off the dying souls around them. There was a song, a jazz song, playing on radio and I remember thinking that this was the greatest song on earth. The song was "Morwa" by Jonas Gwangwa. Morwa means "son" in seSotho. I had never been that much of a jazz fan but I appreciated that song.

Although my friends kept on visiting me there was nothing I wished for more than to see my family. I was the only patient in the ICU who didn't have family by his side and I was dying to see my own family, even though deep down I knew that there was no chance of them coming over to Johannesburg from the Eastern Cape. Every day I wished that my mother would come into the ward, give me a hug and tell me it was all going to be okay. I would often look around and see other patients being comforted by their family members. Needless to say I felt envious.

There was one patient, a middle-aged man, who was often visited by a little girl who I assumed was his grandchild. She would clutch his hand and sing him a lullaby as he lay in his bed. Every time she sang to him, I would feel the tears streaming down my face.

This is something that had never been part of my life before. I had always believed that big boys don't cry, but the macho Thembelani had gone away.

Being far away from home it was difficult for me to know how much of my situation my parents were aware of. I knew that they were in contact with my friends and the nurses, but I didn't know how much they understood of what they were telling them. The phone would ring in the ward sometimes and I would overhear the nurses talking about me. Afterwards a nurse would come and tell me that it was a member of my family. Besides my parents, there were my two cousins, Andile and Zondie, who were calling the hospital every day to enquire about my progress. My father would always want to speak to me over the phone when he called, but the hospital staff wouldn't allow him as I was still in a very critical stage and was not in a position to talk.

During this period the doctors, nurses and even my friends would tell me that I was making progress, but I would never believe them. As far as I was concerned, I was still stuck to that ICU bed with pipes sticking out of my flesh and an oxygen mask covering my face and, in my opinion, that didn't qualify as making progress. However, I kept a brave face and I always smiled at the staff and tried to cheer them up. After all, these people worked with cases like ours every day, and would work with cases like ours for the rest of their lives. The least I could do was to acknowledge their dedication and hard work with a smile.

Four days after the Sunday morning on which I had woken up, the doctor agreed with his staff that they could transfer me to the normal ward. This, I was told, was because I no longer needed intensive care treatment. I was jubilant. This meant I really was making progress. However, there were problems as, for a start, I was still not able to talk properly. I was also unable to lift any of my limbs on my own.

The nurses had told me that after my operation I would have to learn to walk again from scratch. This was bad news but I was happy as they told me that I wouldn't need a wheelchair.

So, although my condition was still bad, I was looking forward to being moved to the normal ward.

On the morning I was supposed to be moved to the ward, two nurses came to my side pushing a wheelchair. Adjusting my bed and reassuring me, they kept telling me how much they were going to miss my small eyes and they asked me to visit their ward whenever I wanted to. I assured them that I would and also told them how much I would miss their soothing hands because I didn't know what kind of treatment to expect on the other side of the hospital. They finally disconnected the machine that I was attached to and waited for a few minutes to check if I coped without it. Then the oxygen mask was removed as well, much to my relief.

I felt even more relieved when they brought me some clean pyjamas to put on. You must remember that, underneath those hospital blankets, I had been naked all along. Being naked didn't make me feel comfortable at all, but when they dressed me and made me ready to move to the new ward I felt so helpless that I wondered if being naked might not be a better option. The long pipe was still inserted in my penis and that also made me feel very uncomfortable. The nurses told me not to tamper with any of the pipes as I was still very delicate and the functioning of my organs depended on them.

The pipe that passed up through my nostril and then back down my throat was still there, irritating as before. My chest was just a zigzag of pipes, each one draining some substance into a pouch. One thing that I surely didn't want to see, I decided as they finished dressing me, was what lay under those big bandages and dressings that covered my chest and the whole of my lower abdomen. I was scared that once I saw what lay beneath them I would lose hope.

Finally it was time for the doctor to examine me one last time before I left. He was full of smiles as he examined me; a clear indication of how satisfied he was with my progress. He never said a word to me though, he just passed on instructions through the nurses. I am sure that he didn't want me to talk as he felt that I would get worse if I talked too much. After he had finished and scribbled something in my folder, I was finally whisked off to the new ward.

On my way out I thanked the nurses and signalled my good-byes to the patients who remained in the ward. Most of them weren't in a position to notice me as they were in the worst conditions that you can imagine, but there was this particular gentleman who looked at me with tears streaming down his face. Apparently he had arrived three days before I had. I smiled back at him and signalled a cross to tell him to trust in God, but then my heart began to feel sore and I didn't look his way again.

Ward 6

I was taken to Ward 6, the ward for the patients that had just come out of the ICU. When I got there my two nurse friends introduced me to the senior nurse in that particular ward. She thanked them and offered to drive my wheelchair into my allocated space. She tried to make me feel comfortable by asking me about my origins and how I ended up in Johannesburg.

It was refreshing to move into a ward with people who were not chained to their beds; it gave me hope, even though I still couldn't get myself out of my bed. The patients in this ward could at least walk, though most still walked with the support of a three-wheeled support apparatus. Just being around people who were recovering made things easier. It gave me hope that maybe one day I would get up from that bed and walk out of the hospital.

The nurse put me in the bed closest to the ward entrance. On my left there was an elderly patient who kept groaning in pain. As I lay there I recalled a story that I had heard from Speech, my friend back in Cape Town. He said that hospital staff put the people who are critically ill and who could die at any moment closest to the door. This, he said, is done in order to quietly whisk them away, should they die, without the other patients noticing. He argued that if they put you somewhere in the middle of the ward, and you passed away, the other patients would lose hope of recovering. But, if they put you closer to the door, no-one would notice if you had been removed dead or alive.

So, here I was, sleeping closest to the door. The nurses knew, I thought, that I might die soon. However, there was nothing I could do about that except to keep praying that God would spare my life and make me better again.

Most of the patients hadn't even noticed me when I was wheeled in; they were too busy nursing their own pain.

I remember looking at this male patient whose throat was stitched. Apparently somebody was trying to slit his throat when his neighbour showed up. The gentleman couldn't even speak. While I was looking at this guy he suddenly looked up at me as if to let me know that I was in a worse situation than he was. I lowered my eyes and concentrated on my own pain.

I stayed in that hospital ward without even attempting to get up until the following day, when I slowly slid out of my bed and tried to stand on my own. After struggling to find my balance for some time I managed to stand. When I realised that I could stand, I became overly ambitious and started to walk slowly towards the bathroom, pushing one of the three-wheeled walkers that had been left next to my bed.

I felt like an old crippled grandfather. One step took a full minute to complete and the bathroom looked more and more distant, but I could walk and that drove me on.

I was still a long, long way from the bathroom when my body gave in and my knees began to shake. I fell down and struggled to get up, until another patient saw me and helped me up and into my bed. The nurses came immediately and rebuked me for trying to walk when I wasn't strong enough. I was told to only attempt walking when there was someone around to monitor me. I duly apologised and lay flat on my bed, exhausted as ever.

The following day I attempted the journey from my bed to the bathroom for a second time. This time I made my way to the bathroom and back with more confidence. Little did I know it then but this was to become my two-hourly exercise routine.

Loneliness was a real problem in hospital. I didn't know anyone on my new ward and I couldn't go back to the ICU and talk to the nurses there. In the end I decided to make the hospital my home because I knew that I was going to spend some time there and, as I adapted to the new routines of Ward 6, I started making friends with both the nurses and my fellow patients. Two of the friends I made were Zizi and Sizwe, both of whom had been admitted two days after I was.

Zizi was my age and had been shot in the chest by his neighbour after an argument about soccer. Zizi had laughed when his neighbour's favourite team had lost and the man had just drawn out his gun and shot him. Just like that.

Everybody had been drunk when it happened so it took a long time to get Zizi to the hospital. He had suffered a lot of internal bleeding and had to have a pipe inserted in his back to drain any blood clots.

His attacker had apparently only realised what he had done the following day. He obviously felt remorse because one day, while we were still in Ward 6, he visited Zizi to ask for his forgiveness. I saw the man enter the ward. He came in with a nervous expression, his hat in his hands as he approached his victim's bed. I studied the man's every move with interest. Was he genuinely remorseful or was he just scared of the consequences of his actions? I wondered. Maybe he was just there to plead with Zizi not to press charges.

Unfortunately for him Zizi was not prepared to talk to him. The nurse on duty duly asked him to leave and he left in shame. How I wished I could have had the opportunity to meet my attackers. It would have helped me heal.

As for Sizwe, he had been involved in a fight over a girl in Thokoza and had been stabbed in the chest. From my conversations with him it was obvious that he was intent on revenge; it was all he and his friends talked about when they visited.

Both Zizi and Sizwe wanted revenge. I often pleaded with them never to follow violence with violence. Zizi was a very funny character and used to call me mfundisi for the sermons that I gave him on this subject.

Another of the patients in Ward 6 was a little guy called Pat, who had had an operation on both of his legs. He had been involved in a serious car accident which had claimed his friend's life, but unlike Zizi and Sizwe he was on the wrong side of the law. Pat and his friend had stolen the car and had hit a lamppost as they tried to flee. The friend, who was driving, died instantly but Pat, who was badly injured, had escaped from the scene. He had been picked up by a motorist and taken to hospital. Here was a criminal who had been lucky enough to get help from the motorist while I, an honest man, had almost died on the roadside. You should know how I felt.

The only good part of his story was his determination to turn over a new leaf, repent and mend his ways. Apparently the death of his friend had affected him and made him want to make a change.

I don't know why Pat had decided to confide in me, but I'm happy he did. Listening to his stories helped me understand the criminal mind a little better and that understanding helped me heal.

In Ward 6 I quickly came to the conclusion that the atmosphere in a hospital is just not conducive to a patient's recovery. Another patient, in the same ward, said that if you put a healthy person in hospital for two days, that person would feel sick, just by being in that environment. In a hospital ward you don't only deal with your own pain and suffering, you also "feel" what the patient next to you feels. This became evident to me one day when they brought a gravely sick woman into the ward and put her in the bed next to mine. She would sob and gasp for the whole night, a clear indication that she was about to die. She would whisper to me to call the nurse, but I couldn't as I could barely speak, let alone shout. I would think about her situation and sob quietly. I think she must have passed away on the second day because they moved her out of the ward while I was still sleeping. You can't imagine how that made me feel, seeing a fellow patient dying in pain.

My friends were still visiting me on a daily basis. One morning Khaya brought my cellphone and told me of all the people who had called to wish me a speedy recovery. I was overwhelmed at the number of people who really cared about me. Some of the people didn't know me well enough to call me a friend, but they called on a daily basis to enquire about my progress. My family, relatives, friends, girlfriend, colleagues and everyone who knew me had called to wish me well. Khaya told me that the phone had been ringing off the hook every day and, as if to prove what he said, it rang as soon as I took it from him.

It was Feziwe, my ex-girlfriend, who screamed her lungs out when she heard my voice. I could hear from the way she spoke that she was in tears, but I tried to comfort her and tell her that I was fine and would be out of hospital soon. When I had finished talking to Feziwe Khaya left for work, promising to visit the following day. This gave me ample time to read all the messages I had on my phone.

I found numerous voice messages on my phone from many different people, some of whom I didn't remember ever having met. There was one voice message from a woman who didn't identify herself but just prayed for me. She must have been one of my parents' friends from church because she referred to me as "Mam'-uNgenelwa's son". I was so touched by all the attention that I broke down and cried. Surely God had blessed me with a lot of caring people. Thank you, Lord.

One morning, my fifth day on the ward, when I could finally walk unaided, I slowly stumbled to the nearest telephone booth to make a call. I put in a five-rand coin and started dialling, hoping that at least one member of my family would be at home.

"Hello," said a voice I recognised as my brother Chuma's. I asked him if my mother was in the house and he called her. I think my brother didn't recognise my voice because he wasn't expecting to talk to me, he probably thought I was just another one of the people who called to enquire about my condition every day. He called my mother and told her there was someone who wanted to speak to her on the phone. I could hear my mother's footsteps over the phone and I couldn't wait to hear her voice. That "Hello" would be enough to make me feel alive again.

When my mother came to the phone she recognised that she knew my voice, despite the fact that it had become so hoarse and deep, and she stopped and asked who I was.

"Thembelani," I replied.

My mother didn't say anything, she just burst into song:

Mazith' iingqondo zethu
Zimbonge uYehova
Kuba iinceba zaKhe
Zimi ngonaphakade

Ezintsizini zethu
Iliso liya bona
Kuba iinceba zaKhe
Zimi ngonaphakade

Kubo bonke oothixo
Akukho onje ngaYe
Kuba iinceba zaKhe
Zimi ngonaphakade

Loosely translated, the song goes:

May our minds
Praise Jehovah
For in our miseries
The eye sees all
Of all the gods
There is no-one like Him
For His grace is forever

This was my mother's favourite hymn. She would sing it every time before she prayed and I had learned to love it as well.

I joined in with the song and we cried together until I ran out of coins and the phone disconnected.

I dragged myself back into the ward. Tears flowing and heart pumping I slid into my bed and spent the whole day crying under the blankets.

Ward 8

As the days went by, the nurses slowly removed the bandages from my body altogether. I have to tell you that I have never been so alarmed in my life. The stitches stretched all the way down from my chest to my pubic area. What made it look worse was the fact that the stitches were made out of wire and looked like staples. It was obvious that I had had serious wounds all over my body and, as soon as I saw the extent of my injuries, I began to weep again like a small child, not out of pain but out of admiration for what God had done for me.

On one of those days, the doctor brought me my X-rays to show me how bad the injuries were. One bullet had missed my spinal column by a mere millimetre. Two other bullets had only just missed my left kidney and my heart. Some of the bullets had broken my ribs. I had been shot once in the chest, twice in the stomach and twice in the back.

The doctor had left but I was still thinking about the X-rays when my phone rang. Whenever my phone rang I would get really excited because it was my only connection to the outside world. My colleagues from Cape Town would take turns in calling me and cheering me up.

I would cover myself with blankets and cry after every call, unable to believe how much people cared for me. I have to say that I always felt ten times better after I had emptied my tears onto my pillow, but I always covered myself so that people wouldn't see me crying. I am a strong African man but I would cry like a little girl whenever I thought about my ordeal and how I had survived it.

I picked up my phone and answered it.

"Hello," said the voice on the other side. It was a female voice and, instead of answering, I tried to guess who it was, but I didn't recognise the voice. "Thembelani, are you there?" the soft voice insisted.

"Hello, yes, I'm here," I said, wondering who it was.

"It's me, Nomaphelo."

"Nomapheeelo!" I felt so overjoyed to hear her voice that I wished I could hug her. "Thank God you are alive. I've been praying every day."

We didn't have time to say much as she sounded as if she was choking on the other side and dropped the phone but, despite this, the phone call had left me the happiest patient in that hospital. Finally, I had heard her voice. She was definitely alive.

She called again the following day and told me about what had happened to her. I had heard some of it from Khaya and Bongani, but she filled in the rest. She told me how she had climbed over the fence into a factory and how scared she had been when the security guards had pointed their guns at her, thinking she was an intruder. After being offered refuge she had lost consciousness for about two hours. When she woke up, she was told that two of her friends had been shot dead. I could feel her pain from the way she spoke. She kept bursting into tears in the middle of her story and I would have to tell her to stop and assure her that I was fine, but in reality the only thing that kept me strong was the knowledge that I had to be strong for her. I was just lucky that she couldn't see my tears as I spoke to her.

The thing that stood out in all my conversations with Nomaphelo was how we both wished we could come together and share our experiences and pain. She told me that she had encountered a lot of problems trying to overcome her ordeal. She once told me of how people didn't believe her when she told them of what she had experienced. She often told me how she wished we could meet. I felt the same. Every time I spoke to her I felt a strong connection. She shared my pain and she felt for me as much as I did for her.

A couple of days after I had first spoken to Nomaphelo, a nurse called me into the visiting room. I will never forget my happiness when I found my father and my cousin Zondie waiting for me. I was still on a drip and I could see that they didn't want to touch me hard in case they damaged something. I couldn't care less about that; I threw myself on both of them. Tears kept streaming down as I hugged my father on the one side and my cousin on the other. It was probably a full minute before we said anything to each other. For the first time in my life I saw a tear drop from my father's eye.

I was reluctant to show them the extent of my injuries, but they insisted on seeing for themselves. It was, they said, the only thing that would allow them to come to terms with my condition. I could see the shock in both their eyes when I lifted my hospital shirt to show them the healing wounds. They stayed for about two hours until I had to be taken back to the ward for some treatment. Seeing that I had made good progress my father and Zondie decided to go back to the Eastern Cape immediately so that Zondie could go to work the following day. They were relieved to see me walking and almost talking properly. However, they left me with an instruction to go straight home to the Eastern Cape after I had been discharged from the hospital.

The following day, I had another special visitor. Mhlabazi, my cousin from Bushbuckridge, had come to see me. She had come to Johannesburg for a nursing course and we had spoken once on the phone about me visiting her in her flat that she shared with her younger brother, Esmile. We hadn't seen each other since 1988, when her family had visited our grandmother in the Trans-kei. The two of us had never thought that we would have our first reunion in a hospital ward, but that's life. She stayed for about three hours but, instead of the joyous laughter of a reunion of cousins, it was all tears.

I had been in hospital for almost two weeks and by this time I was feeling much stronger. My doctor informed me that I would be discharged sometime in the next four or five days, depending on my condition. He advised me to do some exercises – walking up and down one flight of stairs twice a day – to help with my recuperation.

Shortly after this they moved me to Ward 8, a ward for patients that were about to be discharged. It felt even better to be moved together with my two friends, Zizi and Sizwe, who were also go-ing to be discharged in the next few days.

When we got into the ward, we chose three beds so that we wouldn't be far away from each other.

A couple of days after this the doctor informed me that I would be discharged the following day. I was jubilant about finally seeing the outside world again.

On the day that I was discharged from hospital Dr Karera called me aside and sat me down to talk to me. I thought that he had called me aside to give me more instructions about how to take care of myself, or perhaps to tell me about some permanent damage that I had sustained. Fortunately, he wasn't calling me aside for that. The first question he asked was, "Do you believe in God?"

"Yes, I do, Doc," I answered.

He took me back to the day that I had arrived at the hospital with three bullets inside my body and multiple gunshot wounds. He told me that it was only by God's grace that I was alive as the odds were stacked against me. He described my survival as one of the miracles he had seen in his time as a doctor. With a smile, he said, "Whatever religion you believe in, you must go and say 'Thank you' because this really was a miracle."

I didn't know what to say. When I was a young boy in eMadladleni my grandmother was always telling stories of people who had survived tragic vehicle accidents, people who drowned and were feared dead, but who survived, and sometimes of people who had survived mine disasters. My grandmother used to be very good at storytelling, in fact she still is, but when I heard stories like that I always thought that they were too good to be true. Almost all of these "miracles" were said to have happened in distant places and that didn't help me to believe in them. I chose to look at things from a scientific angle and I used to think that the stories she told were simply to make us believe in miracles, to make us believe in religion. I never knew that one day I would experience the power of God first-hand. I thought life was black and white, no grey areas, no hidden truths. I never understood why people, in this day and age, still believed in miracles, but there he was, a medical doctor, not wanting to take any credit for saving the life of a patient and, I thought, if a doctor could say what he had just said, then it really must have been a miracle.

Finally it was time to say goodbye to my fellow patients and the hospital staff. During my time in hospital I had devised various coping mechanisms and I had found that laughter helped a lot. I used to surround myself with the nurses and fellow patients and tell them my hilarious Cape Town stories. I also enjoyed visiting the other wards with more critically ill people to try to give them some comfort. I concerned myself with other people's conditions and this seemed to work wonders for me. I had grown attached to a lot of people at the hospital and it must have taken me about thirty minutes just to wish my fellow patients a speedy recovery.

After saying my goodbyes I went to the storeroom to fetch my belongings. I wasn't sure what condition they would be in. I knew for a fact that Bongani's jacket and my T-shirt had been destroyed. The jacket was in tatters as a result of all the bullets that went through it. As for the T-shirt, they had cut it off my body when I had arrived at the hospital. So I wasn't surprised when they brought me a tiny package containing what remained of my stuff.

I opened the plastic bag to find my tracksuit and shoes, nothing else. When I asked about my other garments, they told me that my T-shirt had been burnt, together with Bongani's tattered jacket.

The tracksuit had a hole in the waist area and it was still soaked in blood. I felt so weak when I realised how bad a condition I had been in when I was admitted to the hospital. I reached for the tracksuit pockets to see if there was anything in them. Guess what? A ten-rand note together with a dry cleaner's slip. It was evidence that I hadn't been searched at all, I was just brutally attacked.

"Are you okay?" asked the gentleman who had handed over my things.

"I'm fine," I said, thanking him and making my way to the records department to collect a doctor's certificate.

In the records department waiting room I opened my file and went over what had really happened to me once I had arrived at the hospital. I was petrified when I saw that the operation had started at 23:45 and ended at 02:55. Major surgery had been carried out on my stomach, colon, small bowel, jejunum and liver. Three hours and ten minutes with my chest and stomach cut open? Equally scary was the realisation that I had only been operated on two hours after my admission.

Bongani was waiting for me in the hospital waiting room. Together, we headed for the taxi rank and took a taxi to Germiston as I had decided to spend a night at Khaya's flat before going home to the Eastern Cape to be with my family.

We got out at the Germiston taxi rank and went down Station Road to Pirrowville. It was at that moment that the memories came flooding back. I was about to walk towards the very road that we had used on the day of the horror. I could already see Linton Jones Road branching off from the street that I was walking down. I looked at Bongani and noticed that he was feeling the same way. We didn't say anything about it, we just grasped each other's hands and nodded our heads.

That moment felt like a new beginning in my life, it was as if I was reborn into the world. As soon as we arrived at the flat I locked myself in the bedroom and prayed.

That night I began to realise the psychological effects of my accident. I dreamed that these thugs had followed me from the hospital to Germiston and that they were all pointing guns at me, telling me that I wasn't safe yet. They said they wanted me dead. They had covered their faces and I couldn't see them, I could just see their scary eyes. In the dream I screamed my lungs out and every time I screamed, my wounds would feel as if they were being cut open again.

I woke up sweating, with tears in my eyes. Fortunately I hadn't woken Khaya. I was so scared that the tears kept pouring out of my eyes, even after I had woken up and realised that it was only a dream. I forced my eyes open so that I wouldn't fall asleep and dream the same dream again. In fact, I stayed awake until the break of dawn when my friends woke up to prepare for work. I couldn't wait to get home, to my parents. I would feel safer there, I thought.

Going home, alive

At six the following evening I was in a City to City bus at Johannesburg Park station, waiting for the driver to start the engine and take me to Engcobo. There I was going back to my place of birth with the complete opposite of what I had expected to go home with. I hadn't found a job, instead my body was covered with bullet wounds that were still healing; I couldn't bend, I couldn't talk properly, I couldn't walk fast, I couldn't even bathe myself. I had tears in my eyes and nothing in my pockets. But I was still breathing. I still had life. My body might have felt numb, but my heart couldn't wait to get to Engcobo. When the bus conductor announced over the loudspeaker that the bus was about to depart, I slowly lifted my tired body and hugged both Khaya and Bongani. We said a short prayer together and they got off the bus, wishing me a good journey. I waved back at them and said, softly, "God bless."

After they got out of the bus they stood next to my window. I nodded my head and smiled. Khaya, in particular, had seemed troubled by my departure, but I had reassured him that I would be fine.

The bus started to move slowly as the onlookers waved to their loved ones. Even though the others were dispersing, my friends were still sadly staring at the bus and waving. Finally they disappeared from view as the bus moved out onto the main road.

It was only then that I started to look around at the passengers. There was an elderly gentleman with a hat in the seat next to me, who reminded me of my uncle. The man had nice grey hair and a few gracious wrinkles on his face. Clearly he had lived his life long enough to see his grandchildren grow up. He looked at me as if he could hear what I was thinking and nodded his head.

"Kunjani, tata?" I asked, trying to start up a conversation.

"Sikhona, mfana," the man responded.

I glanced forward to look at the other passengers. There were two middle-aged ladies in the seat in front of me, but I couldn't see who was behind me as I still had trouble turning my head. I turned back to the man to continue with our little conversation but was quickly disturbed by my cellphone.

"Hello," I picked it up.

"Who's speaking?" a voice asked from the other end.

"Thembelani," I answered, still puzzled at this caller who had demanded to know who was speaking even though he was the one who had called my number.

"Thembelani . . . But . . . they said . . ."

It was Mlu, my long-lost high school friend who had heard the rumours that I had been shot dead in Johannesburg. He had wanted to verify it for himself, so he couldn't believe it when I answered the phone. I told him the whole story and informed him that I was indeed alive and was on my way to Engcobo to stay with my family for a while.

He told me that many people believed the stories and assumed that I was dead already. He had received a call from one of our neighbours at home to tell him of my death and he told me that many people from my village were certain that I had passed away and were getting ready to attend my funeral. Obviously the gossip-mongers had got it all wrong. I told him to spread the word to those who knew me and tell them I was alive.

I had barely put the phone down when a lady in the seat in front of me turned around and started talking to me. She had been listening in on my conversation with Mlu. She was one of the Natalspruit Hospital staff, on her way home for a holiday, and she straightaway asked if I was the same person that she had seen in hospital. I told her that I was and she introduced herself to me as one of the nurses who had welcomed me on my arrival at the hospital. She started to tell me about my condition during sur-gery as she had been present during the operation. She told me about my shattered liver, my destroyed intestines and about how many bullets they had retrieved from inside my body.

Apparently the doctor was about to stitch me up when they discovered one last bullet that was lodged somewhere between my ribs. It was then that it all made sense; I understood why I had heard a voice saying, "Not another one!"

She also told me about how much I had kept moving during the surgery, when I was supposed to be sedated. I tried to be strong as she was telling me all this, but my emotions were just beyond my control and the tears streamed down my face once again.

All this time the gentleman next to me had his mouth ajar with amazement and before I knew it I was surrounded by a small audience. I quickly stopped talking to the nurse and looked out of the window. We were hardly out of Gauteng and still had a long journey ahead of us; I didn't want to be the centre of attention all the way to Engcobo.

We stopped for a few minutes in Vereeniging for the bus to re-fuel but I didn't get off with the other people in case they started to ask me questions about my time in hospital.

As the bus continued on its way I dozed off and only woke up when we were approaching Barkley East. I knew we weren't that far from Engcobo. I tapped the nurse on the shoulder and asked her how far we still had to travel. She said we'd be in Queenstown at about three in the morning. I figured out that I would arrive in Engcobo roughly three hours later. We talked all the way until she had to get off in Cofimvaba.

About twenty minutes after we had left Cofimvaba I saw E-ngcobo from a distance. The morning mist was slowly making way for the sun and the small rural town seemed to be waiting just for me. I could see some people driving a span of oxen, whistling joyously. The grass was green after the spring rains and the live-stock looked in good health. I breathed a sigh of relief as the bus crossed the Umgwali river and headed into town. I knew I was home, back where my umbilical cord was buried. This was what I had longed for while I had been in hospital. It was good to come back alive, not in a black coffin, as we used to say in my place.

When I finally arrived in my home town I was so tired that I knew I couldn't walk. I asked the bus driver to drop me next to the taxi rank. When I got there I sat under a tree, said a little prayer and waited for the first taxi to come. I knew from my conversation with Mlu that many people thought I had passed away in Johan-nesburg and so I decided I would try to avoid as many people as possible. I was still sitting there, trying to avoid people, when I heard a familiar female voice. "Umntwan'am," the sweet voice said, "Thixo, Umkhulu!"

I slowly turned around to find my mother running towards me. She had decided to come and wait for me in town instead of waiting at home. I tried to stop my tears and smiled. "Mama, mama," was all I could manage, as I saw the strange mixture of pain and excitement on my mother's face.

This was the first time I had called her "mama". I had grown up calling her "sisi", emulating her sister who had stayed with us while I was young. But that morning I called her "mama" for the first time.

We embraced. I felt the warmth of her hug and the comfort of her shoulder. Her tears dripped continuously as she mumbled a short prayer. That moment is still with me every time I think of her.

After that she took my bag in one hand and my hand in the other and we made our way to the taxi that was waiting.

When we reached eMadladleni we got out at the bus stop near the shop. There were a number of people waiting for the bus and everyone looked at me with awe. I saw some familiar faces and waved my hand to greet them. It was at that moment that one elderly woman started to ululate and a male voice shouted, "You have defeated death and the devil, my boy, your ancestors have been looking after you."

I turned around, bowed my head in acknowledgement and continued walking home.

When we got home, my father was standing at the entrance of

the kraal, waiting for us. He looked on appreciatively as I slowly walked towards him and stretched out his hand to greet me. There were tears in my father's eyes. Shaking hands proved not to be enough. We hugged. The three of us went inside. I was told that my two younger brothers were at school and would be home that afternoon. Shortly after that, my grandmother came in and gave me a hug and a kiss on my forehead. I felt like a five-year-old again. It felt good to be home, well and alive.

My family all gathered for a prayer service to thank the Lord for my survival. Throughout the prayer service I couldn't say a single word, I was crying non-stop. The emotions were overwhelming.

A few minutes after the prayer my brothers, Chuma and Mandisi, came in. I could see the pain in their eyes as they took turns greeting me. I guess it hurt them to see me in such a condition. I didn't say a word, just spread my arms and hugged them both at the same time.

In the first week that I stayed at home, life was very challenging. I couldn't eat solids, I couldn't walk for further than four hundred metres and I couldn't bathe myself. I was still experiencing some pain in my abdomen and back; they had operated on my liver and the pain from around my liver would become excruciating when I walked quickly or coughed. The wound in my chest was also a problem; it didn't look like it was going to heal anytime soon. When I removed the dressings from it I would see some pus and just lose hope. What if there was some kind of permanent damage? Would I ever live a normal life again?

Living on a special diet of juice and yoghurt was also very challenging in a place where stamped maize and beans is the staple food. I was dependent on my family for almost everything, which was very difficult for a person who had been very independent almost all his life.

Despite these frustrations and fears I was also touched by the many people who came to visit me to congratulate me on my survival and to say a prayer for me. Prayers became the order of the day.

Life was just so beautiful to me. I was seeing everything in a different light and I became more in touch with my spiritual side.

However, there were also funny episodes. Every day I would walk to the nearest shop to get exercise, and I remember this one day when my cousin came with me to buy some bread. When we arrived at the shop – which also doubles up as a shebeen – we were confronted with some patrons, most of whom were drunk. One older woman looked at me and screamed: "A ghost! A ghost! Malusi's son's ghost!"

I couldn't help laughing at how scared they were. My cousin had to calm the women down, telling them that I wasn't dead.

It must have been my third day at home when I removed the bandage on my stomach and realised that the wound had become infected. The stitches had loosened and there was watery fluid coming out of the wound. I felt pain as soon as the wound came in contact with the air and started to fear the worst. What if the wound wouldn't heal?

The next day I went to the local clinic where they drained the fluid and gave me some antibiotics. A day later, the wound started to heal again.

It didn't take too long to recover after that and after spending two weeks at home, enjoying the care my family lavished on me, I was able to eat normal food and I could bend a little. When I realised that I was able to do some things on my own I knew it was time for me to go back to work in Cape Town. My family were still worried about whether I was ready to go, but I reassured them that staying alone wouldn't be too much of a problem as I was able to dress my wounds and cleanse them. But, no matter how much I tried to convince them that I would be fine on my own, they still didn't believe me.

I was willing to put everything that had happened behind me and live my life once more. I wanted to forget about the incident and just move on. My parents both told me not to hold any grudges and to accept what had happened as the will of God. They also told me to forgive the man who had done this thing to me.

It was a Thursday when I decided to take the bus back to Cape Town and start working again. I knew my colleagues would give me the support that I needed. I had received calls of encouragement every day while I had been in eMadladleni. For the first time in my life both of my parents accompanied me to town. They had begun to accept my decision and they understood my desire to continue with my life and forget about what had happened.

I told myself that I would live my life in Cape Town as if nothing had happened. I told myself that I was going to put on a brave face in public and avoid talking about my experience. Little did I know that just about everyone who knew me knew what had happened. Some thought I was dead already, some had heard that I was in a wheelchair and very few knew the correct details.

The bus arrived in Cape Town in the early hours of Friday morning. It was a warm spring day and my love for Cape Town was instantly renewed as I looked up and saw Table Mountain. What a view!

When I finally got home I must have stood for at least fifteen minutes outside the flat just enjoying the morning, marvelling at the familiar chant of the taxi drivers and the beauty of the Cape.

Inside the flat I carefully took my clothes off and snuck under my blankets. It felt so good to be in familiar surroundings that I fell asleep straight away.

I woke up hours later when I thought I heard a knock on the door. I uncovered my head and listened closely. The soft knock sounded again, and I slowly got off the bed and made my way to answer the door. It was Cynthia, my girlfriend. She had sneaked out of her class to come and see me. Tears streamed out of her eyes as we looked at each other, unable to say a word.

"Y-y-you are . . ." she stuttered as she tried to control her emotions. I guess she wanted to be strong for me, but it was proving to be difficult not to cry.

"It's okay," I said. "It's me, and I am alive and well and waiting for my hug".

As I looked at her, I saw such a mixture of emotions: she had a smile on her face, but her tearful eyes showed pain and sadness. She wrapped her hands around me and gave me the warmest embrace. Time stood still and everything around us ceased to exist. We dragged each other into my room and closed the door behind us.

An hour later, I took a shower and made my way to work where I had heard they would be having a farewell meal for one of my colleagues, Mbhedesho, who had found another job in Johannesburg. We were a very close-knit team and we made a point of organising a party every time one of our colleagues celebrated their birthday or got another job. I had decided that this gathering would be good for me because I would see all of my colleagues at the same time and would be able to tell the story once and spare myself the pain of having to repeat the same story over and over again.

When I got to the venue I tried to make a quiet entrance and attract as little attention as possible, but as soon as my colleagues spotted me they all got up and took turns shaking my hand and hugging me. I struggled to hold back my tears as I thought about how important they all were to me. I thanked each and every one of them for all their support and prayers and went on to tell them what had happened and pleaded with them to treat me the same way they did before my ordeal.

I was touched when Mbhedesho finished his farewell speech by saying that he felt honoured to see for himself the miracle that had happened in my life. This dude was never a sentimental person, but on that day everything he said came straight from his heart despite the fact that his farewell party had almost turned into my welcome home party.

After all the formalities Tahirih dragged me aside to show me a printout of the last email I had sent to her before I had left for Jozi. Even when I read it I thought it sounded like a letter from a person who knows they are about to die. I had signed it off with: "With love and respect, till we meet again, so long."

Tahirih is a very spiritual person who is part of an Interfaith

102

association. She only said a few words to me but they went a long way to helping me heal. She said, "Thembelani, what happened, happened and for a reason. Do not ask God 'Why?' He knows what He's doing. We are all just happy that you survived."

I spent the rest of the day with my colleagues until it was time to go home. Shirleen, my colleague with whom I shared an office, offered to walk me home, as she didn't want me to travel alone. On our way she had asked if, given a chance, I would avenge myself. "Never," I said. "I would just ask them the reasons why they did this thing to me and after that I would be willing to forgive them. I am at peace."

She looked me in the eye and embraced me. She was still concerned about the condition I was in, but it had felt good to be part of the team again and I was ready to start work the following Monday despite my boss, Karolina, telling me to take another week off. People didn't understand that the more I stayed home the more depressed I felt. I was yearning for some kind of routine to keep my mind busy. I was tired of the self-pity that engulfed me when I was on my own; I wanted to get everything back to normal. I was back and ready for life.

The suspects

When I got out of the hospital I had expected my story to be covered in all the newspapers and magazines. However, the newspapers were more concerned with sports stories and politics and the magazines were more interested in celebrity scandals. My story of survival didn't make the pages of the local media. Not that I was looking for any publicity, far from it, all I needed was closure, but I thought that if people read about my plight those of them with relevant information would come forward and help the police with the investigation. Of course this only would have worked if there had been an investigation in the first place. The fact is that for a long time I didn't know if the police had actually investigated my case at all. I had expected someone from the police service to come and interview me while I was in hospital so that they could open the investigation, but it never happened.

In the end it turned out that my friends hadn't been patient enough to officially open a case with the police; there was just no time for that. The important thing for my friends at the time was to locate me and save me from the thugs. The police told them that they weren't able to help them with this as they didn't have a vehicle, so Khaya and Bongani had rounded up their friends and neighbours and made their own search party.

After I had learned this I called the Germiston police station to try and find out if anything had ever happened and I was told that the police didn't know a thing about it because nobody had opened a docket for that crime. Things were also complicated by the fact that after coming out of the hospital I had gone straight home without going to the police first. At the time all I wanted was to go home and be with my family. I had assumed that someone had opened an investigation, but in reality the suspects are probably still roaming the streets of Germiston, beating their chests about how they once killed an "enemy". I wish I knew what had happened to them.

During my first few months back in Cape Town I saw my attackers in my dreams almost every night. In those nightmares they were boasting about how they had shot me and how much they would love to do it again. They would threaten me and poke my dripping wounds with guns and knives. Their faces, though, would change every time.

I was also still asking myself the same questions that had been in the back of my mind all along: Why was I shot in the first place? I just couldn't deal with this question. There were too many unknowns to ponder: Was I the original target of these people? Had I offended them in some way during our first encounter? Did I look threatening to them? Did I look like someone else that they knew? Were they trying to shoot someone else but ended up shooting me by mistake and decided to finish me off just for the fun of it? Were they testing their shooting skills in preparation for some fight? Did they know that they had almost killed an innocent man? Did they care?

In my quest to try and find closure I wanted to put names to those cruel faces. In the end, having no other way of doing this, I decided to give them fictitious names so that I could identify them. I thought that if I treated them like human beings I would find some answers. I wanted to be able to say, "So-and-so tried to kill me".

Initially, I wanted to name them Devil, Dragon, Evil, Demon and Killer, but I decided otherwise. I told myself that I had to remember that these men were someone's beloved children, someone's beloved brothers and some were probably someone's fathers. Because of this I wanted to give them decent names. The fictitious names I came up with were: Tshepo, Sipho, Mandla and John. The fifth one, my attacker, I decided to call Saul. I wanted to give him a biblical name that belonged to someone who used to oppress and harm the Israelites but one day was changed and became a God-fearing man. I had this strange hope that maybe this man would one day think about all the evil things that he had done and change his ways. I was praying for his salvation. If what he did to me was the last atrocity he committed then I would be a happy man.

As for the other criminals, Tshepo, Sipho, Mandla and John, I felt nothing but pity for them. Maybe they were good-natured human beings who happened to mix with the wrong crowd. Maybe they came from broken homes where they were never taught the value of human life. Maybe they came from poor families and poverty had turned them into monsters that killed to find some fulfilment. But then how many black people were there who knew nothing about poverty? I wasn't sure if this was a reason for anyone to do what they did to me. There is always the excuse among black criminals that poverty drives them to commit crime, but this wasn't a case of people stealing bread from a shop. I don't believe poverty would drive anyone to shoot at an unarmed stranger five times and dump him on the railway lines. I thought this was simply a matter of people who lacked any regard for the law and who didn't value human life.

The politicians would probably blame it on the legacy of apartheid, but again, that is not an excuse. I grew up under the same system, in the same circumstances as them, probably even in a worse situation than they had. I also refuse to blame crime on the government; they don't occupy people's hearts and minds. Government makes and passes laws; it is up to the people to obey those laws.

Back in my childhood I knew of children who followed what their peers did, good or bad. These kids would never initiate anything by themselves; they always succumbed to peer pressure and always wanted to be with the in crowd. I just hope and pray that they will one day change their ways and find it in their hearts to ask for forgiveness from all the people they hurt and from God.

I was trying in my own way to find closure as there was no chance of me ever meeting these people and getting them to give me their reasons of why they had done this thing to me. I was desperate for explanations. I never wanted revenge. If they had come to me and asked for forgiveness, explaining their reasons in all sincerity, I would have had no choice but to forgive them.

Eventually I came to the conclusion that it is the kind of society we live in that makes this life painful. Human beings don't know or care about the meaning of life. This doesn't only apply to criminals like Saul and his friends. It is the same uncaring attitude that makes people, like my friends Zizi and Sizwe from Ward 6, think that revenge is acceptable. It is the same uncaring attitude that allows people to buy stolen goods from murderers without worrying about who has been killed to get those goods. Our society worships local gangsters because of their wealth, forgetting how that wealth was obtained in the first place. Big-shot gangsters get given appreciative nicknames by our communities. The same communities know who the criminals are, where they stay and what kinds of crimes they're involved in, but they never do anything about it. A criminal is someone's brother, cousin or neighbour, but in our communities these people are never confronted.

Underlying this problem is the fact that parents in our communities have abandoned their responsibilities. Some parents suspect that their children are involved in crime but never do anything about it.

I remember when I grew up my parents would never allow me to wander about at night. We never owned any weapons, including knives, because my parents took an active role in my upbringing and ensured that we followed the right path. They were involved in our day-to-day lives and taught us to control our emotions and actions. Even our neighbours did everything they could to steer us from the wrong path.

Nowadays, some parents don't see anything wrong in letting their children wander the streets at night. By the time those kids get older they don't have any values. Some children even grow up in the shebeens, where the patrons fight and stab each other while the onlookers cheer them on.

We cannot expect the police alone to stop crime, the parents and communities must participate. I cannot blame the police for what happened to me, they cannot be expected to guard each and every citizen all the time. I can only blame society. Human life has become so cheap in South Africa that people are no longer enraged about the violent crime covered in the newspapers, they just turn to the sports pages. People have given up. Gone are the days when criminals only stole and left you to live; nowadays they kill you before searching you. I am a living proof of what many South Africans have experienced at the hands of ruthless criminals. My case is not exclusive; it is just one of many. I still think about the middle-aged man who was killed the same day I was attacked. I often wonder how his family are coping without their breadwinner. What he died for, his family will never know.

These days I am not even sure if my attackers still remember what they did to me. To them it is probably just one of many things that they have done to many people. As Saul said, I was like a stray dog that he didn't care about.

I cannot begin to try and understand his actions. What I know is that he shot me five times and left me to die alone on the railway lines and that he did all of this without any provocation. The wounds may have turned into scars and the pain may have turned into memory, but I will never take what happened to me for granted. I will never again take life for granted. I will forever owe my life to the way God saved me that day. My miraculous survival will occupy my mind until the day I finally die.

The aftermath

My wounds were beginning to heal but the trauma was becoming worse by the day.

As you know I had been ordered by my boss to stay at home for at least a week. She didn't think that I was in the right state of mind to come back to work, but I wanted to reclaim my life as soon as possible.

I had dropped in at work about three days after the party to catch up with my colleagues and was on my way home when this man approached me. In fact, it is not accurate to say he approached me as he was going his own way. I had seen this man on campus before but on that day he looked different and I noticed instantly that he was wearing almost the same outfit as Saul had worn the day he attacked me. He was wearing a maroon T-shirt and khaki pants. As he approached he put his hand into his pocket, presumably to take out a pen or something. As soon as he did that the memories flashed in front of my eyes and it seemed to me as if he was about to take out a gun. I could hear the guns in Germiston. My heart raced and I was suddenly sweating. My knees felt so weak. I started shaking and fell down.

I must have lost consciousness for a while because when I got up I was sobbing and there were tears in my eyes. My clothes were soiled from lying on the ground and there was a man standing by my side asking me if I was okay.

Feeling scared I told him what had just happened and he helped me to my flat. After I got into my flat I closed the doors and started praying. I must say, though, it was very difficult to pray because I ended up sobbing so heavily that I couldn't mutter a single word.

Unfortunately, though, that wasn't the end of the trauma. I would feel scared every time I came into contact with this guy and, as he was a student at UWC, this was quite a regular occurrence. I am sure that he resembled Saul because after that first traumatic encounter I felt the same about him every time I saw him, even if he was wearing different clothes.

In the end I even resorted to introducing myself to him. I wanted to face him and talk to him so that he wouldn't traumatise me any more. After all, he wasn't the one who attacked me, he just resembled him.

At the same time as I was struggling to deal with the student who looked like Saul, I was also having the same nightmares I had been having ever since I had come back to Cape Town. The fact that I was staying alone in a flat didn't help either as there was no-one to comfort me when I had the nightmares. I would wake up shaking at night and switch on the lights. Even though there was no-one else in the room I would feel as if someone was stalking me. I would even imagine that I could hear footsteps. My only consolation was that I was free to cry openly. In the end I even resorted to sleeping with the lights on.

In addition to my nightmares I was scared of anything to do with guns. I remember one day when Cynthia and I went to watch a movie in Century City mall. By that time I thought that I was strong enough to watch any kind of a movie. But, just to be safe, I carefully chose a comedy. Right towards the end of the movie, in one scene, I saw a gun. Initially I didn't have a problem with it and I thought I would be strong enough to watch it. I stayed put. But, alas, I lost it when one character started shooting another. What made it unbearable was the way that scene resembled my ordeal. He was shooting him while he was down and there was blood all over the place. The body of the victim kept jerking up and down as the gunshots kept sounding and, unbelievably, the whole scene took place close to the railway tracks.

I hadn't realised that I was crying so loudly until the lights came on and Cynthia was trying to comfort me while everybody else watched us. I felt so embarrassed.

Cynthia helped me back to my flat where I just covered myself with a blanket and cried.

Guns were not the only cause of my despair. The way the motorists passed by while I was dying on the side of the road was another bitter pill to swallow. I can never, ever forget the speed at which they passed by. Worst of them all was that brown van that even tried to run me over instead of helping me out. Every time I thought of that van, I started trembling. The driver went out of his way to try and knock me down. The things that people do to fight criminals!

One of the hardest blows to take was when one of my uncles approached my mother at a funeral and told her that I was probably shot because I had slept with somebody's wife or because I had been doing some dishonest things. He even questioned the fact that nobody was arrested for shooting me. He said this at a funeral in front of the other mourners and my mother's friends. He had also claimed that I might have been drunk and provoked my attackers. People would never just attack an innocent person, he told her. My mother had to lock herself away in an empty room to cry.

Imagine this coming from a person who calls me his nephew. I must say I had expected some people to think that way because they didn't know what had really happened, but my uncle was one of the first people we had told about it. Strangers were very sympathetic to my plight, but a close relative made a joke out of it. I haven't spoken to him since.

This experience has made me think of the thousands who have fallen victim to these senseless crimes. Some have lost their lives and some have been paralysed and some, like me, will forever live a life of trauma. There are so many people out there who will never get any closure as nobody will ever come forward to claim responsibility.

After trying and failing to analyse and understand my tragedy and my subsequent survival, I had resolved to believe that God wanted to show His miracles and that He had decided to use me. I took it upon myself to reclaim my life, not as a victim of crime but as a victor. I decided to live my life to the full and dedicate all my life to realising the purpose that God wanted me to serve in this life. I now realise that I am a special person. I might not have money and all the material things that I had always dreamed of having, but I have the most important gift of them all – I have my life.

The new life

I was back in beautiful Cape Town and starting to pick up the pieces of my life. My job contract had been extended for another year and I thought that things were starting to look promising. All of a sudden I had started to appreciate everything that I had. My girlfriend and my friends in Johannesburg were providing me with all the love and support I needed and I was starting to heal. I was able to walk longer distances and I could even run for a short distance. I had also become even closer to God, ever grateful for each day that passed, and aware of how He loved me as His son. Hope was becoming reality.

In the meantime I had become something of an attraction at the flats where I lived. Every day I would get people coming to hear my story and see the miracle for themselves. Most of them would tell me that I would be blessed with a long and fruitful life after all I had gone through. They were always surprised to find me in good spirits. Some wouldn't even believe that I was the same person they had heard about until I showed them the scars. I even received an unexpected visit from a long-lost ex-girlfriend who had heard my story through a mutual friend. It was humbling to know how my life had touched so many people.

At the end of that year I moved into a flat in Bellville. My relationship with God had become a very close one. I had joined the Methodist Church and I was enjoying my life again.

Fast-forward to Monday, 11 October 2004, exactly a year after my ordeal. I was in a hospital theatre again, this time in Mitchells Plain, Cape Town, and all around me were theatre staff in their green uniforms. I had my eyes closed and my body was trembling. My heart was beating fast and warm tears were pouring from the corners of my eyes as I clutched at a jerking hand.

The difference this time was that the doctor wasn't operating on me. Minutes later, I heard a cry that overwhelmed me. Cynthia and I had been blessed with a beautiful little girl with my nose and my ears and, fortunately, her mother's eyes. Tears of joy streamed down my cheeks as I closed my eyes one more time to make a little prayer. A new life was born.

Cynthia and I named her Emihle to acknowledge the beautiful miracle that she is.

Acknowledgements

To God the Almighty: thank you for the miracle.

I would like to send my sincere gratitude to Doctor Gerard Karera and all the Natalspruit Hospital staff for all that they did for me. I would also like to pass on my heartfelt gratitude to the three gentlemen who picked me up by the side of the road and organised some help – I hope one day I'll shake your hands and say "Thank you" in person.

To my friends, Khaya Bolosha and Bongani Msuthu, thank you for filling the missing spaces and may God bless you. Also many thanks to Cynthia for giving me strength when I was down. Simphiwe Nelana, thank you for the encouragement. My mentor and friend, Diana Ferrus, thank you for the inspiration.

To the Kwela Books family, especially Nicola, thank you for the guidance.

Post-traumatic Stress Disorder

_by Dr Soraya Seedat, psychiatrist and co-director of
the Medical Research Council Unit on Anxiety Disorders_

Thembelani's heartfelt account is a reminder of how no-one is completely protected from traumatic experiences – trauma happens to many strong and healthy people. By trying to understand trauma we can be less fearful of it and manage it better. Thembelani's overwhelming fear during the shooting and his continued mental and physical reactions to reminders of the incident constitute a common effect of traumatic experience known as post-traumatic stress disorder. It is clear that his inner resolve, the care, concern and understanding from the hospital staff and the support of friends, family and community were critical in lessening the painful effects of his experience and in promoting his recovery.

Description

- Post-traumatic stress disorder, or PTSD, is a condition that can develop following the experience or witnessing of traumatic events.
- These include natural disasters, acts of terrorism (such as bomb blasts) and physical assault (such as rape). In South Africa, PTSD is a common condition in the context of violent crimes, such as hijackings and shootings, violence encountered during housebreaking, sexual assault and domestic violence.

- The person encountering the traumatic event doesn't have to be the one who was threatened directly. He or she can also be a witness.
- Most survivors of trauma return to normal given a little time. This is true in Thembelani's case. However, some people will have stress reactions that do not go away on their own, or may even get worse over time.
- Symptoms must last for at least a month after the traumatic event for a diagnosis of PTSD to be made.
- PTSD is complicated by the fact that it often occurs together with other disorders such as depression, substance abuse and physical or mental health problems.

People who have the condition:
- experience intense fear, helplessness or horror at the time of the trauma
- persistently have upsetting memories, thoughts or images about the trauma
- feel as if the trauma is happening to them again (flashbacks)
- have bad dreams and nightmares
- become upset when reminded of the trauma
- avoid thoughts, feelings, places and activities that remind them of the trauma
- have trouble remembering important parts of the event
- feel disconnected from people and the world around them
- feel emotionally "shut down" and have difficulty showing strong emotions
- feel little hope for their future

- lose interest in activities they previously enjoyed
- have trouble sleeping
- feel shaky and sweaty
- constantly feel unsafe and on the lookout for danger
- become very startled by loud noises.

Cause

The exact cause of PTSD remains unknown. However, it is agreed that a defining factor is that a person with PTSD must have experienced a profoundly distressing event. In addition, we now know that there are clear biological changes that are associated with PTSD.

The disorder tends to be more severe when the trauma involves deliberate human malice, as in Thembelani's experience, as opposed to a "twist of fate" or bad luck. But because not all people who experience a serious trauma develop PTSD, other factors such as previous trauma and the absence of social support may play a role in the development of the disorder.

Symptoms

The symptoms of PTSD fall into three categories:

1. Intrusion

Memories of the trauma occur unexpectedly, and episodes called "flashbacks" intrude into a person's day-to-day routine. This happens in sudden, vivid memories accompanied by painful emotions that hold the victim's attention completely. The flashbacks may be so strong that individuals almost feel as if they are experiencing the trauma again or seeing it unfold before their eyes. They may also have nightmares of the traumatic incident.

2. *Avoidance*

Avoidance symptoms often affect relationships with others: the person with PTSD often avoids close emotional ties with family, colleagues and friends. At first, the person feels emotionally numb and can complete only routine, mechanical activities. Later, when re-experiencing the event, the person may alternate between a flood of emotions caused by re-experiencing the trauma and an inability to feel or express emotions at all. The person with PTSD avoids situations or activities that are reminders of the original traumatic event because this may cause symptoms to get worse. He or she may show less interest in things they used to enjoy doing. Depression is a common product of not being able to process painful feelings. Fortunately, Thembelani was able to work through his. Some people also feel guilty because they have survived the trauma while others – particularly friends or family – did not.

3. *Hyperarousal*

PTSD can cause a person to act as if he/she is constantly being threatened. A person with PTSD can become suddenly irritable or explosive, even when not provoked. Getting into arguments and fights with people is not uncommon. The constant feeling that danger is near causes exaggerated reactions. Many people with PTSD also attempt to rid themselves of their painful re-experiences, loneliness and panic attacks by abusing alcohol or other drugs as "self-medication".

Course

The response to a traumatic event normally occurs in three phases. A person is more than likely experiencing PTSD *only* when the symptoms of phase one and two persist beyond four to six weeks. PTSD usually appears within three months after a trauma, but may appear later.

Phase One – Impact Phase (first few days after the trauma)
- Feeling shock
- Feeling emotionally numb
- Feeling disconnected
- Feeling panicky and anxious
- Feeling regressed and helpless

Phase Two – Recoil Phase (lasts two to four weeks)
- Mood swings (anger, sadness, anxiety)
- Flashbacks and repeated thoughts such as "Am I going crazy?"
- The person begins to adapt

Phase Three – Reorganisation Phase
- Symptoms subside
- Social and work functioning begin to improve

When to see a doctor

Not everyone who experiences trauma requires treatment. Like Thembelani, some recover with the help of family, friends or clergy. But many do need professional treatment to recover from the psychological damage that can result from experiencing, witnessing or participating in an overwhelmingly traumatic event. Having post-traumatic symptoms does not mean that a person has PTSD. If a person is experiencing symptoms that are either causing distress or getting in the way of their work or home life, he/she should be assessed by a GP, psychiatrist or psychologist. Should traumatic stress symptoms persist beyond four to six weeks, therapy and medication may be necessary.

Treatment

If you have suffered a trauma and recognise that you have symptoms of PTSD, then the following practical guidelines may be helpful:

- Remove yourself from exposure to further trauma if possible, i.e. stabilise your situation. (This may not be as simple as it sounds – for example if you are a policeman/woman or a paramedic. Regular trauma debriefing by a qualified professional every time a trauma has been witnessed should prevent the development of PTSD.)
- Find a therapist who has experience in treating PTSD and, preferably, who is knowledgeable about the kind of trauma you have experienced. Be truthful with your therapist about your experience and symptoms. If you feel that the therapist is not right for you, you have the right to one that is. You also have the right to a second opinion.
- Consult a psychiatrist to determine if you would benefit from medication.
- Have a medical doctor examine you for any additional medical problems.
- Avoid unhealthy behaviour and coping addictions, drug and non-drug alike.

- Find a support group for people with PTSD.
- Remove yourself from people and situations that are not supportive.
- Learn about PTSD by reading about it and talking to health professionals and other people who have had the condition.

Medication

The most common type of medication prescribed for PTSD is antidepressants. Antidepressant medications are often particularly helpful in treating the symptoms of PTSD. Sertraline (Zoloft) and paroxetine (Aropax) are licensed for the treatment of PTSD in some countries. Because they are probably not helpful and because of the risk of addiction, benzodiazepines (also known as "tranquillisers") should be avoided or used very judiciously. A psychiatrist should carefully monitor medication. Medication can take up to a few weeks to take effect and must not be stopped suddenly.

Medication is often used in conjunction with therapy. The relief from symptoms that medication provides allows most patients to participate more effectively in psychotherapy. Treatment for PTSD may last for one to two years or longer.

Therapy

Psychiatrists and other mental health professionals also use a variety of effective therapies to help people with PTSD work through their trauma and pain. Behaviour therapy focuses on correcting the painful and dysfunctional thoughts and behaviours by teaching relaxation techniques. Discussion groups or peer-counselling groups encourage survivors of similar traumatic events to share their experiences and reactions to them.

Children and trauma

Even though young children may not fully understand the context of what is happening to them and around them, they are nonetheless sensitive to changes in their world and respond to change in significant people such as parents and to changes in their environment, routine and emotional climate.

Trauma, if untreated, can have lasting effects on the child's personality development. While the child may not have the cognitive capacity to understand or remember an incident, the trauma may still have an impact on him or her.

Children, despite their resilience, may not necessarily get over a trauma without some form of treatment. There is not uncommonly a discrepancy between the adult's perception of the child's vulnerability and the child's report of their own reactions. A lack of observable behaviour or symptoms doesn't mean that the child has come to terms with the trauma. When a child has experienced a traumatic event, it is important to allow him or her to talk about what happened, to "speak about the unspeakable". Parents often need support too and it is therefore recommended that both child and parents seek professional help.

Adapted and revised from an article appearing on health24.com

Helpline numbers

Bathuthuzele Youth Stress Clinic   021 938 9162
  (specifically for adolescents of   021 938 9018
  12–18 years with PTSD)

Centre for the Study of Violence and   011 403 5102
Reconciliation Trauma Clinic

Depression and Anxiety Group helpline   011 783 1474/6

Lifeline   0861 322 322

Mental Health Information Centre   021 938 9229
(MHIC) of South Africa

Trauma Centre   021 465 7373

Further information

Mental Health Information Centre (MHIC) of South
Africa: www.mentalhealthsa.co.za